The Scottish Borders
40 favourite walks

D1334739

The author and publisher have made every effort to ensure that the information in this publication is accurate, and accept no responsibility whatsoever for any loss, injury or inconvenience experienced by any person or persons whilst using this book.

'Breathes there the man with soul so dead, Who never to himself hath said,
This is my own, my native land!'
– Sir Walter Scott

For Tom, Wilfie and Neil

published by
pocket mountains ltd
The Old Church, Annanside, Moffat DG10 9HB
pocketmountains.com

ISBN: 978-1-907025-50-1

Text and photography copyright © Robbie Porteous

The right of Robbie Porteous to be identified as the Author of this work has been asserted by him in accordance with the Copyright, Designs and Patents Act 1988

A catalogue record for this book is available from the British Library

Contains Ordnance Survey data © Crown copyright and database right 2016, supported by out of copyright mapping 1945-1961

All rights reserved. No part of this publication may be reproduced, stored in a retrieval system, or transmitted in any form or by any means, electronic or mechanical, including photocopying and recording, unless expressly permitted by Pocket Mountains Ltd.

Printed in Poland

Introduction

The Scottish Borders cover a vast area, stretching from the rugged east coast to rural Dumfriesshire and from the more populous Lothians to the border with England. Although there are no very high mountains in the Southern Uplands, the Borders have always attracted walkers keen to explore the varied countryside, scenery and topography found here, as well as the fascinating ruins of abbeys and castles, the grand estates and the rich literary heritage of the area. There are also several long-distance walking trails which traverse the region, including The Southern Upland Way, The Borders Abbeys Way, St Cuthbert's Way and the Berwickshire Coastal Path, which link together many Border towns.

This guide contains 40 routes, the majority offering easy to moderate walks, with a few more challenging hikes to the top of higher hills. There is no claim to be comprehensive; the walks selected here are merely a sample of what is possible.

The routes are divided into five sections. The first features walks along the east coast and inland towards Lauder; the second explores the Upper Tweed Valley from West Linton and Broughton down towards Galashiels; the third centres around the Ettrick Forest, the ancient royal hunting ground west of Selkirk; the fourth takes in the area around the four abbey towns of Melrose, Kelso, Jedburgh and Dryburgh; the final section looks to quiet Teviotdale and Liddesdale south of the largest Border town of Hawick.

Safety

The geography of the Borders means that different weather conditions often prevail in different parts of the region, so be prepared for every eventuality, particularly on longer walks over higher ground.

Sturdy walking shoes or boots are recommended for all routes. The majority follow good paths and tracks, but in some cases the terrain can be boggy. Take wind- and waterproof clothing and ensure you have enough warm layers to enjoy the walk whatever the conditions.

The sketch map accompanying each route is intended to help plan the outing rather than as a navigational aid. The relevant Ordnance Survey Explorer or Landranger map should always be taken. On longer routes that cross open ground, a compass and the knowledge to use it is a very useful thing.

Some of the walks include sections along high and unfenced cliffs where special care should be taken, especially if you have children or a dog with you.

Access

Although the main towns and larger villages in the Borders are well served by buses, there are many areas which are sparsely populated and less easy to reach without a car. While every effort has been made to include walks that can be reached by bus, this guide would be incomplete without routes in the harder-to-reach spots. Several of the walks utilise old railway beds; happily a section of one of them has been recently reopened, providing a link from Edinburgh to Tweedbank, north of Galashiels. Details of public transport in the region can be found at www.travelinescotland.com.

Responsible walking

While the Borders countryside is a great resource for outdoor activities like walking and cycling, it also provides a living for many farmers and foresters. To avoid conflict between walkers and those who work the land, it is important to enjoy the great outdoors responsibly.

Walkers in Scotland have long enjoyed the right to roam on just about any land with no requirements to stay on defined paths or rights of way. This position was clarified by the Land Reform (Scotland) Act 2003 which gives everyone the right to access most land for purposes of recreation, provided they act responsibly.

Always follow the Scottish Outdoor Access Code. Some of the walks in this guide cross land where farm animals graze or deer and groundnesting birds live. If you take a dog, it is very important to keep it on a lead in such areas.

Occasionally you may encounter temporary access restrictions. This could, for example, be a forest track closed due to tree harvesting or a path shut because of erosion. Usually a diversion will be offered and if this is the case you should follow it. If there is no diversion, you may have to consult your map and work out an alternative route.

Wildlife

With its landscape of high moorland, lochs, woodland and coast, the Borders offer a diverse natural habitat for a wide variety of animals, birds, insects and plants.

St Abbs on the east coast of Scotland is well-known for the thousands of fulmars, razorbills, kittiwakes, shags and puffins found here. Inland, the region's small lochs attract ducks, swans and grebes and some also see visiting greylag and pink-footed geese. You may also spot heron and osprey fishing in the rivers and streams. Other birds of prey such as buzzards, kestrels and sparrowhawks hunt over the high moorlands which are also home to golden plover, curlew, meadow pipit, wheatear and mountain hare. Reclusive red squirrels and roe deer thrive in the mixed woodlands throughout the Borders.

During the spawning season you will also see salmon leaping up the cauld as they make their way up the Yarrow Water and the River Tweed to complete their epic journey to breed.

History

The Romans arrived in the south of Scotland around 80AD and, after coming to terms with the local tribes, the Votadini and the Selgovae, built a network of roads and forts. Their largest encampment, known as Trimontium, was sited in the shadow of the three Eildon Hills at Newstead, near Melrose. Finding the rest of the country harder to conquer, however, they withdrew south to build a great wall from the mouth of the River Tyne to Carlisle. Without realising it, Hadrian's

Wall sparked the notion of two separate parts of Britain, with Alba – later Scotland – a distinct entity on the other side of that symbolic barrier.

Over the following centuries, the people of the borderlands prospered and the stability of the region allowed for the building of four magnificent abbeys at Jedburgh, Melrose, Dryburgh and Kelso during the reign of David I. The booming wool trade with the Continent, through the port of Berwick-upon-Tweed, also led to the exchange of culture and ideas between Europe and Scotland in this golden era.

Things changed with the accidental death of Scotland's heirless King Alexander III in 1286. A prolonged and costly civil war between Scotland and England followed in which the biggest casualties were the people and economy of the Borders.

During the Wars of Independence both Robert the Bruce and William Wallace used the Ettrick Forest near Selkirk as a base from which to attack the English. Independence was finally won at Bannockburn near Stirling in 1314, but the relationship between the crowns was never easy. Two centuries later, the disastrous Battle of Flodden near Coldstream saw the slaughter of thousands of young borderers and the resumption of hostilities which only ended with the Union of Crowns under James VI in 1603.

While royal authority was weak and marauding armies devastated the region, many local families took to stealing cattle and sheep and plundering everything they could from villages and towns throughout the Scottish Marches and down into Northumberland and Yorkshire. The Reivers, as they came to be known, rode through the darkest nights and owed no allegiance to their country or warring kings. These violent times left a legacy of castles and fortified towers, as well as adding the words 'bereavement' and 'blackmail' to the English language.

It is often said that this tumultuous history shaped the character of the typical borderer; strongly determined to remain independent and proud of what is theirs.

Oral history was also important to the borderers' sense of identity and there was a strong tradition of balladry and of romantic stories being recited by the firesides in farmsteads and villages. These old tales inspired two great writers, the 'Ettrick Shepherd', James Hogg, and Sir Walter Scott, and it was Scott who created much of the popular perception of Border history which persists today.

The rapid development of the textile industry in the 19th and 20th centuries saw the rise of Galashiels on Gala Water, Hawick on the Teviot and Selkirk on the Tweed, all drawing workers off the farms and into the mills. Land remains important to Borderers, however, and they remember their shared past in the annual Common Ridings which date back to the Middle Ages when young men, known as in these parts as 'callants', would ride out to secure their town boundaries. In many ways the Borders also remain a region apart, a cherished land full of history, character, beauty and romance.

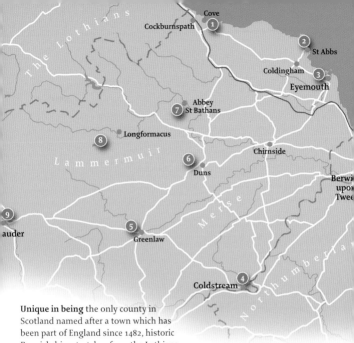

Unique in being the only county in Scotland named after a town which has been part of England since 1482, historic Berwickshire stretches from the Lothians in the north to the River Tweed and the border with England in the south, and from the royal burgh of Lauder in the west all the way to the east coast.

Agriculture in the fertile plain known as the Merse, sheepfarming on the rolling Lammermuir and fishing from Eyemouth have long been important to the local economy. The towns central to these activities – Duns, Lauder, Coldstream, St Abbs and Eyemouth – are all vibrant places with proud histories which enjoy wonderful settings.

The first walks in this chapter follow sections of the Berwickshire Coastal Path

which extends from Cockburnspath down to Berwick-upon-Tweed. Heading inland, the next walks explore a grand estate near Coldstream, an unusual hillfort near the former county town of Greenlaw and an historic hill with a great view near Duns.

On the edge of the Lammermuir, the next walk features a rare isolated ruin, and the final two routes both take the high road over quiet moorland utilising sections of the cross-country Southern Upland Way and the old 'Herring Road' which once linked the Berwickshire coast to the market town of Lauder.

Coldingham Beach ▶

Berwickshire and the east coast

Cove to Siccar Point

Distance 11km **Time** 2 hours 30 (out and back) **Terrain** clifftop path, often muddy and partly unfenced, and tarmac road **Map** OS Explorer 346 **Access** the nearest bus stops at Cockburnspath, 1.5km from the start

This out-and-back clifftop walk, much of it on the Berwickshire Coastal Path and Southern Upland Way, visits the rocky promontory of Siccar Point made famous by the 'Father of Modern Geology', Edinburgh-born James Hutton.

The walk begins from the car park at Cove, just off the A1 near Cockburnspath. Eleven men from Cove lost their lives in the Great East Coast Fishing Disaster of 1881, and a poignant sculpture by Jill Watson overlooks the sea from the side of the car park.

Two paths go south from the car park – this walk follows the one on the right, signposted for the Berwickshire Coastal Path and the Southern Upland Way. The other path leads down to Cove's natural harbour and it is worth making the short detour to explore the unusual hand-excavated cellars and the tunnel which gives access to this privately-owned idyll before returning to the car park.

Back on the clifftop, a great view of the harbour can be enjoyed as you make your way along the unfenced path (which can get muddy). A natural sandstone arch known as the Hollow Rock and a sea stack are also soon passed as you head towards the east coast surfers' haven of Pease Bay.

As you near the chalets of Pease Bay, the path joins a minor road; follow this down to a ford and bridge, ignoring the Southern

◄ Cove Harbour

Upland Way path which heads off over a stile to the right. Cross over the bridge and walk up the road until you reach a fenced path off to the left which takes you back up to the clifftop.

The path carries on farmland to reach a minor road which accesses a vegetable distribution warehouse. Turn left and follow the road until you come to an information board and small car park. Cross a stile and walk around the edge of the fields, passing the ruins of 16th-century St Helen's Church on the left as you make your way to the information boards above Siccar Point.

This section of coastline is famous in the history of geology as a result of a boat trip in 1788 taken by James Hutton. At Siccar Point he observed the angular unconformity which proved his theory of geological development. Gently sloping strata of Devonian Old Red Sandstone overlie almost vertical layers of much older Silurian Greywacke; profound evidence that our planet was created over an unimaginable period of time, not the few thousand years that was previously thought. As Hutton's companion in the boat, John Playfair, later observed; 'the mind seemed to grow giddy by looking so far into the abyss of time'.

There is a faint path leading sharply down to the sea from the information boards; there is no need to go this way. Instead follow the wall round to the right to get a better view before returning to Cove and the start by the same paths.

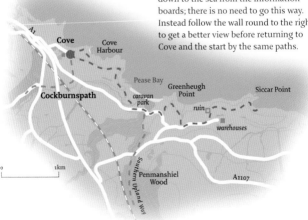

St Abb's Head circular

Distance 7km **Time** 2 hours
Terrain minor road, grassy paths and
tracks; beware of the very high cliffs!
Map OS Explorer 346 **Access** regular buses
from Berwick and Edinburgh to St Abbs

Thousands of nesting kittiwakes,
guillemots, razorbills, fulmars, shags,
shearwaters, skuas and puffins and other
migrating birds populate the high cliffs,
seastacks and marshland on the craggy
headland north of St Abbs on the
Berwickshire coast, making this National
Nature Reserve a mecca for birdwatchers
and wildlife lovers. This walk through
countryside and over the spectacular
clifftops never disappoints.

From the entrance to the National Trust
for Scotland car park (charge for non-
members) found just off the B6438 on the
road down to St Abbs Harbour, turn right
and go past Northfield Farm. Continue
past a row of estate houses and stay with
the lighthouse road, ignoring all other
tracks until you reach a left-hand bend.

Leave the road here and carry straight on
down the signposted track to the Mire
Loch, a 660m-long freshwater lake. Make
your way along the reed- and gorse-fringed
bank to the far end, listening and looking
out for the various grebes, heron, swan,
moorhen and warblers that call this home.
Up ahead, the old jetty at Pettico Wick is
where supplies for the lighthouse keepers
at St Abb's Head were landed before the
road was built.

Just after the car park for disabled
visitors, leave the road by the rough path
which goes sharply up onto the clifftops.
Take care when you get to the top and stay

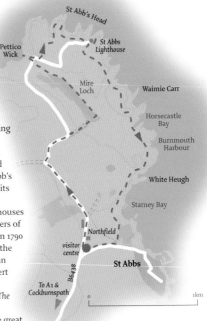

◀ St Abbs from the lighthouse path

well away from the edge of the cliffs (this section can be avoided by staying with the road all the way to the lighthouse). Make your way along the various grassy paths, enjoying the exhilarating views before rejoining the road near the lighthouse.

Built by brothers David and Thomas Stevenson, the St Abb's Head Lighthouse first shone its light in 1862 and is one of a remarkable 97 manned lighthouses designed and built by members of the Stevenson family between 1790 and 1940. The black sheep of the family who did not become an engineer was, of course, Robert Louis Stevenson, author of *Kidnapped*, *Treasure Island* and *The Strange Case of Dr Jekyll & Mr Hyde*, although he did take great pride in his family's achievements. As he wrote to his publisher, 'all the sea lights in Scotland are signed with our name – I might write books till 1900 and not serve humanity so well'.

Carry on around the lighthouse walls, perhaps detouring to visit the huge foghorn, before enjoying the scenery and birdlife as you head along the path towards St Abbs.

There are a number of interesting old shipwrecks off this stretch of coast and several boats regularly take divers out from St Abbs Harbour.

When you reach a gate you can either head back to the National Trust for Scotland car park and tearoom or go left to explore the fishing village. If you do choose to visit St Abbs, just above the harbour you will find an excellent visitor centre (free admission) with some great artifacts and old photographs of the area.

11

Eyemouth to Coldingham Priory

Distance 8km **Time** 2 hours (out and back) **Terrain** clifftop paths and country lanes **Map** OS Explorer 346 **Access** regular buses link Eyemouth and Coldingham

This route follows the Berwickshire Coastal Path from the port of Eyemouth to Coldingham Priory, an important holy site founded by St Aebbe the Elder in the 7th century, before catching a bus back to the start.

Start the walk from the shorefront Leisure Centre in Eyemouth and take the waymarked path which leads up to the clifftop holiday chalets. The chalets are soon left behind as the path carries on around Killiedraught Bay. The path is muddy in places but easy to follow as it winds around the clifftop before dropping down to cross a small footbridge in Hallydown Dean.

Further on, the quiet beach at Linkim is a great spot for beachcombing. Keep on the path to climb up and over the promontory of Yellow Craig Head to reach another quiet little beach with Milldown Burn at its northern end. Cross the footbridge and go up the steps to reach Homeli Knoll at the southern end of Coldingham Sands, a Blue Flag beach popular with families and hardy surfers.

The Berwickshire Coastal Path carries on around the bay, passing a beach café, toilet block and a colourful row of shoogly beach huts, some of which are said to be over 100 years old.

Leave the beach by climbing up the sandy steps and pass The Kip, a huge seastack which stands sentinel at the north end of the bay, as you make your way to St Abbs, a fishing community once known as Coldingham Shore.

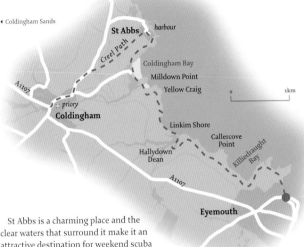

◀ Coldingham Sands

St Abbs

harbour

Creel Path

Coldingham Bay

Milldown Point

Yellow Craig

A1107

priory

Coldingham

Linkim Shore

Callercove Point

Killiedraught Bay

Hallydown Dean

A1107

Eyemouth

0   1km

St Abbs is a charming place and the clear waters that surround it make it an attractive destination for weekend scuba divers. Britain's first voluntary marine reserve was established here in 1984.

After exploring the harbour and visiting the excellent new information centre located in the old town hall, follow Creel Road to reach the signposted Creel Path. Before St Abbs was established, this was the most direct route for the fishermen of Coldingham to get to their lobster pots, or creels, as they are known locally. The path leads between the hedgerows to join the minor road into Coldingham.

On reaching the road, turn left and follow the pavement into Coldingham, passing Fishers Brae on your right as you make your way up to the wooden bus shelter at the top of the High Street.

If you have time before your bus arrives

make your way to the grounds of the nearby Priory. The history of this site is fascinating; described as a 'Monastery of Virgins' by Bede, the original building was burnt down and rebuilt in 679 before being destroyed again by Danes in 870. It lay in ruins until 1098 when it was re-established as a Benedictine Priory before being partly burnt down once more in 1403 and sacked by passing English armies in 1537 and 1547, and again in 1560 during the Scottish Reformation. It was finally finished off by Oliver Cromwell in 1650. Some of the old Priory walls have been incorporated into the present church building which dates from the 1850s.

Coldstream and The Hirsel

Distance 9km **Time** 2 hours 30
Terrain woodland and riverside paths
Map OS Explorer 339 **Access** regular bus
from Berwick to Coldstream

**This circular walk from Coldstream
follows the River Tweed before visiting
the grounds of the welcoming Hirsel
Estate. The estate is home to various craft
shops, as well as a café and a museum,
and there are several options for shorter
walks or variations of this one.**

From the Home car park next to the
Castle Hotel, turn right on Coldstream's
High Street (A698) and carry on over the
bridge. Before you reach the driveway to
the Hirsel Estate look out for the stone
pillars at the entrance to the Lees Estate
on the left-hand side. Go up the drive
initially, then follow the path to the right
round behind the tennis court and
through the woodland.

At the riverside turn left to visit the Lees

Temple, a fenced-off but still lovely
octagonal 18th-century gazebo which
looks down on one of the Tweed's most
venerated fishing spots, the 'Temple Pool'.

Retrace your steps along the Tweed and
continue on the riverside path, looking
out for oystercatchers and heron as you
go. When the path joins a farm road make
your way up past Fireburnmill Farm and
the old mill cottages to the A698. Take care
crossing the road and enter Dundock
Wood at its corner on the other side.

At the next junction of paths go left and
make your way through the trees. In 1870
hundreds of cartloads of peat were
brought down to the estate from the
Lammermuir Hills to provide the right
conditions in which to grow acid-soil-
loving rhododendron and azalea. The
collection in the woodland is seen at its
best in late May or early June.

Keep right on the woodland path to
shadow the south bank of the Hirsel Lake

◄ Lees Temple overlooking the Tweed

and pass a hide on the way towards the courtyard which houses the visitor facilities and craft studios. Turn left on the road in front of the courtyard and then left again at the next junction to enjoy a long view of Hirsel House (not open to the public).

The Hirsel has been the seat of the Earls of Home since the 17th century and the earliest parts of the house date from then. When the 11th Earl married Lady Lucy Elizabeth Montague Douglas in 1832, his estate was amalgamated with that of the illustrious Douglas family. The present Earl is the son of Sir Alec Douglas-Home, the 14th Earl of Home, who gave up the title in 1963 to serve as Prime Minister.

Carry on along the road and turn right at the next junction, then go past the stables before bearing left to join 'Montague Avenue', the old main approach road to Hirsel House which follows the course of the Leet Water. Look out for the Cow Arch which provided access to the riverside pastures for the Hirsel herd of cows as you follow the road around.

At the next crossroads, turn right and cross the Dunglass Bridge over the Leet, then turn back south along the riverside path. Follow this all the way back down the river and through the golf course to reach the car park at the Castle Hotel.

Greenlaw Dean and the Blackcastle Rings

Distance 8km **Time** 2 hours
Terrain tracks and paths, often muddy
Map OS Explorer 339 **Access** regular buses
from Galashiels, Berwick and Kelso stop
in Greenlaw

**This short but adventurous walk follows
the Blackadder Water from the historic
village of Greenlaw through a steep-
sided, secluded valley to explore an
unusual Iron Age promontory fort in the
foothills of the Lammermuir.**

Until Duns took over the role in 1904,
Greenlaw was the county town of
Berwickshire and most of the fine
architecture in the town dates from those
days. For this walk, park near Greenlaw's
magnificent town hall and cross Duns
Road towards the Blackadder Holiday
Park. Pass the Old Town Jail, now a private
house, on your right as you enter the
caravan park.

Follow the main drive through the
caravans with the Blackadder on your left
until you reach a wooden gate which leads
into woodland. Keep on the riverside path
which makes its way up Greenlaw Dean to
reach a bridge. Go up the steps, turn right
on the concrete farm road and go through
the gate on the left to continue on the
riverside path.

Looking out for herons taking off and
landing by the Blackadder, keep following
the river by the narrow and sometimes
muddy path as it winds its way along the
valley floor. Eventually you arrive at the
Deil's Neuk – a steep-sided cut into the
right-hand embankment overlooked by a
stand of Scots pine.

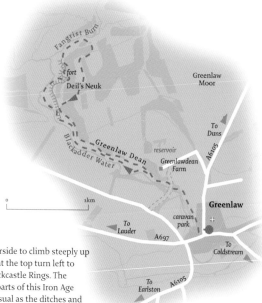

Leave the riverside to climb steeply up the ravine and at the top turn left to explore the Blackcastle Rings. The earthwork ramparts of this Iron Age hillfort are unusual as the ditches and embankments provide protection on one side and the steep drops down to the Fangrist Burn and the Blackadder Water protect the other two sides of the spur.

From the fort there is a view over the confluence of the Blackadder Water and the Fangrist Burn and north over Dogden Moss. Following Fangrist Burn north would take you to the Kaims Esker, a long gravel ridge, up to 15m high in places, left behind by melting glacial rivers around 12,000 years ago.

For this walk, however, continue north and then northeast along the top of the embankment before turning south at a wide break in the forestry plantation. Follow the path through fields bounded by the plantation and keep bearing right through the breaks in the trees until you loop back round to join a path above the route taken earlier. Follow this higher path above the Blackadder before rejoining the lower path at a break in the embankment.

Return to the bridge over the Blackadder crossed earlier and make your way back through the caravan park to the start.

Duns Law and Hen Poo

Distance 7km **Time** 2 hours
Terrain woodland, good tracks and paths
Map OS Explorer 346 **Access** regular buses
from Coldstream and Berwick to Duns

Starting with a short climb to the top of
Duns Law above Duns, the historic county
town of Berwickshire, this easy circular
walk goes on to explore the nature
reserve in the peaceful grounds of the
Neo-Gothic Duns Castle.

From the centre of Duns, make your way
to the archway entrance to the grounds of
Duns Castle. The path up through
woodland to the 218m-high summit of
Duns Law appears on the right of the drive
almost immediately and it isn't long
before a gate is reached. Go through this
and head right to enjoy an expansive view
over Duns, the Cheviots and, on a good

day, Holy Island off the Northumbrian
coast. There is an orientation board with
information about the history of the site
and the view.

Turn around and look for the fenced-off
Covenanters' Stone which marks the spot
where General Alexander Leslie raised the
Covenanters' standard in 1639 in defiance
of King Charles I's imposition of
Episcopalianism on his Scottish subjects.
Leslie's army, which numbered over 12,000
men, made their camp on Duns Law and
took their oaths of allegiance to the
Scottish Kirk here.

Leave the summit by the gate and turn
right to follow a path down through
woodland, then make your way across a
meadow to reach an estate road by the
side of Hen Poo, a charmingly named
man-made loch. Duns Castle sits at the far

end of the loch which was dug as part of the landscaping works commissioned by the Hay family in the 18th century. Look out for the mute swans and various species of duck which make Hen Poo their home, as well as visiting pochard and goosander.

Turn right along the road, go past a private driveway and continue along the main track to reach the Mill Dam which once helped power the estate sawmill. Follow the signpost for the Colonel's Walk and leave the main track before crossing a small footbridge. Keep following the signs for Duns as you make your way through the nature reserve.

Continue to pass a cottage and bear right at the next junction to walk down the estate road past Duns Castle which sits in beautiful parkland to the left.

When you reach the main road into Duns (A6105), turn left and pass between the old and new high schools as you make your way back into town along the pavement.

On the way you will pass the Jim Clark Room, a museum dedicated to one of Formula One's greatest drivers. Having started his career driving in rallies and hill climb events around Berwickshire, Clark went on to win 25 Grand Prix races and two World Championships before his death in a crash at Hockenheim in Germany in 1968.

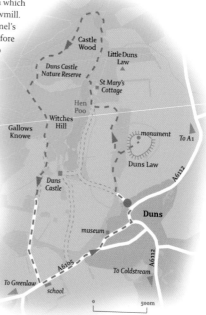

◀ Duns Castle from Duns Law

Edin's Hall Broch

Distance 10km **Time** 3 hours 30
Terrain riverside paths and farm tracks,
final section on minor roads
Map OS Explorer 346 **Access** no public
transport to the start

Emerging in the Iron Age around
2300 years ago, brochs were large
drystone roundhouses unique to
Scotland. Around 570 sites have so far
been identified, from Galloway to
Shetland, but the intriguing Edin's Hall is
one of only a handful found outwith the
Highlands and Islands. It is a great
centrepiece to an enjoyable circular walk
which starts from the quiet village of
Abbey St Bathans.

Park by the river on the right-hand side
of the car park at the Riverside Restaurant

in Abbey St Bathans and follow the
riverside path to emerge onto the minor
road to Duns. Turn left to pass the timber
yard and arrive at 'Toot Corner'. Take the
path signposted for Edin's Hall Broch into
the woodland and then traverse the open
lower slopes of Cockburn Law. The
unusual Retreat House, a circular late 18th-
century hunting lodge built by the Earl of
Wemyss, can soon be spotted on the far
side of the Whiteadder Water.

The path continues to a signpost
pointing off to the summit of Cockburn
Law – a worthwhile diversion on a clear
day – and Edin's Hall Broch. Carry on
downhill and go over the stile.

The size of the broch (nearly 28m wide),
and the quality of its construction, comes
as a pleasant surprise. Thought to have

been built between the two periods of Roman occupation of Scotland on the site of an older hillfort, the original purpose of Edin's Hall remains a mystery, although it is more likely that it was built for tribal prestige than for defence or refuge. In its original state, with its massive 'cooling tower' walls reaching into the sky, it would certainly have been an awesome sight. The only broch still with its walls intact to their full height is on Mousa in the Shetland Islands.

After exploring the broch, follow the vintage Historic Scotland signs in reverse and shadow the Whiteadder Water,

passing through gates and over stiles, before dropping down to the riverside to eventually cross the Elba Footbridge suspended over a scenic gorge.

On the other side, follow the track through woodland before turning left on a minor road. Carry on along the tarmac up the hill until you reach the turning for Blackerstone and The Retreat. Take this road, and, when it forks left, carry straight on along the track. Approaching the river, leave the track on a signposted path into woodland to find a footbridge and ford. Cross over the river and return to the car park.

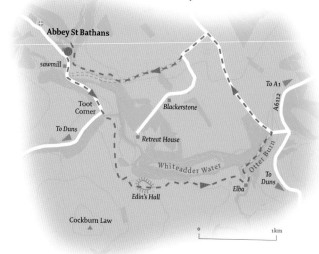

The Twa Brithers o' Twin Law

Distance **10km** Time **3 hours (out and back)**
Terrain **farm tracks and hillpaths**
Map **OS Explorer 345** Access **no public transport to the start**

This walk follows the Southern Upland Way to visit an unusual pair of hilltop cairns high up in the Lammermuir Hills. There are few distinctive peaks in this expansive moorland barrier between East Lothian and the Borders and care needs to be taken as low cloud and mist can make navigation difficult.

The Watch Water Reservoir is reached by single-track road from the village of Longformacus which sits on the Dye Water west of Duns. The access road passes a water treatment plant and goes through a farm. (There is a gate here; remember to close it after driving through.)

The parking area by the fishery lodge is well used by anglers on the reservoir, so please ask for permission before leaving your car here.

From the car park, follow the tarmac road across a cattle grid and on through a pasture to reach Scarlaw Farm sitting above the far end of the reservoir. Carry on past the farm buildings to reach a wider road recently upgraded to provide access for windfarm maintenance. Look out for the Southern Upland Way marker posts and follow them south along the gravel road and over the wooden bridge at Twinlaw Ford.

This track was once more commonly known as the 'Herring Road', along which salted fish were carried in creels from Dunbar to Lauder. Continue along this until another SUW marker post directs you to the right on a wide well-made track. From here it is a straightforward, gradual climb with improving views all the way to the summit of Twin Law.

◀ The Twinlaw Cairns

The story behind the striking cairns on the summit concerns two twin brothers, supposedly buried here beneath the stones. Separated as children, they grew up to become soldiers in opposing Scots and Saxon armies. During a battle fought on a nearby hillside, both were mortally wounded and were buried together when their commanders discovered their connection. A ballad verse on the white trig post sitting between the two cairns also commemorates the 'twa brithers'.

During the Second World War, the cairns were used as target practice and substantially damaged by British and Polish tank operators in training. They were expertly repaired when the war ended by a team of local drystane dykers,

and both cairns now have small alcove shelters which are a great place to sit and enjoy the view over the Eildon Hills and the Cheviots away to the south.

Unless you feel like carrying on to reach Lauder by the Southern Upland Way, turn around and use the same path to return to the reservoir and the start.

On the way back, look out for a stone marker post on the left-hand side of the road near Twinlaw Ford. The stone is inscribed, 'There is no water on the Lammermuir sweeter than at John Dippies Well, Keeper, Rawburn 1865-1897' – the water may indeed be sweet, but it's also where the gamekeeper stashed his whisky!

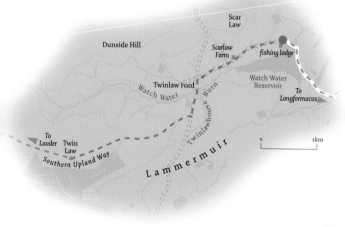

Dabshead Hill and the Lambs' Moor

Distance 20km **Time** 5 hours
Terrain farm and forest roads and good
paths **Maps** OS Explorer 345 and 338
Access regular bus services from
Edinburgh stop in Lauder

Starting from the market town of
Lauder, this challenging route follows
the Southern Upland Way over exposed
moorland to reach a remote cottage,
before returning to town via
the summit of Dabshead Hill on the
western fringe of the Lammermuir.

From the Market Place in Lauder follow
the Southern Upland Way signs south
along the A68 until you reach an opening
in the high wall on the left, just after the
police station. This leads down into the
grounds of Thirlestane Castle which can
soon be seen peeking over the treetops.

Until the end of the 16th century the
Maitland family resided at Old Thirlestane
castle, the ruins of which can be found
3km east of Lauder. The much more
impressive present castle was established
in 1590 by Sir John Maitland and

remodelled in the 1670s by Sir William
Bruce, the man who introduced classical
architecture to Scotland.

Cross over the Leader Water and leave the
castle behind as you follow the SUW
markers around the field edge and up the
hill into woodland. Take the clear path
through the trees before turning right on a
track to reach the busy A697. Cross the road
and make your way up the access road to
Wanton Walls Farm. Go through the farm
and keep heading uphill to pass the
waterworks building before entering the
plantation. Keep with the SUW and go over
the stiles before dropping down to cross the
Snawdon Burn.

After the next stile, bear right and climb
uphill again, before dropping down to the
Blythe Water. Cross the footbridge and head
towards the Scoured Rig plantation where
the access track to the remote cottage at
Braidshawrig is met. Follow this towards

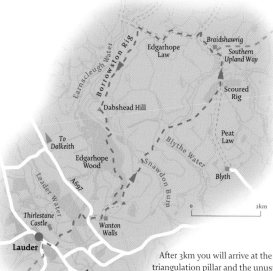

Map labels:
- Earnscleugh Water
- Borrowston Rig
- Edgarhope Law
- Braidshawrig
- Southern Upland Way
- Scoured Rig
- Dabshead Hill
- Peat Law
- To Dalkeith
- Edgarhope Wood
- Blythe Water
- Snawdon Burn
- Blyth
- Leader Water
- A697
- Thirlestane Castle
- Wanton Walls
- **Lauder**
- A68
- To Earlston
- 0   2km

the cottage and sheep pens and then leave the SUW to cross the bridge.

Pass the sheds and keep on the main track, with the burn down to your left. At the next junction make a sharp left turn and follow the track down to cross the water. The track rises again over the flank of Edgarhope Law and bears right at the next five-way junction. Keep with the main track and as it begins to drop steeply make a sharp left turn to the southwest along the top of Borrowston Rig and the escarpment which overlooks the Earnscleugh Water.

After 3km you will arrive at the triangulation pillar and the unusual 'lang stane' summit marker of Dabshead Hill. This is not an ancient standing, or even leaning, stone, but was erected to celebrate Lady Mary Maitland's marriage in 1845.

Return to Lauder by going down through the ditches left by the Iron Age people who once occupied a hillfort on this site and pick up the track running alongside the forestry. With the large pond on your left, look for a wooden gate into Edgarhope Wood on your right and go down through the trees to meet a wider track. This leads back to the junction passed earlier and the SUW signpost. Follow your outward route from here back to Wanton Walls and on to Lauder and the start.

◀ The summit of Dabshead Hill

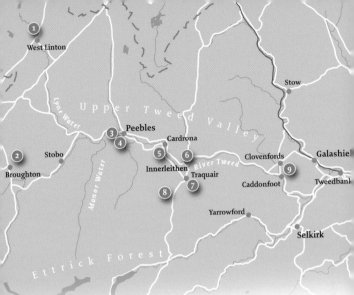

Although it's only the fourth longest river in Scotland, the Tweed can lay a good claim to being the most beautiful as it winds its way through some of the country's most bucolic scenery. In its upper section, from its source at Tweed's Well near Moffat to its meeting with the Yarrow and Gala Waters, it is also one of the fastest-flowing. This power was harnessed at Innerleithen and Walkerburn by the woollen mills which brought great prosperity to the area in the 19th century.

The main town of the Upper Tweed, however, is the charming Peebles. A popular tourist destination since Victorian times with strong literary associations, in more recent times it has become the mountain-biking capital of Scotland; the nearby Forestry Commission-run centre in Glentress Forest attracts keen riders from all over Britain and beyond.

As well as biking trails there are miles of great hillpaths and riverside tracks to enjoy in this area. The first two walks begin near the Lyne Water and the Biggar Water, both tributaries of the Tweed, and the Tweed is then followed in the next walk which utilises an old railway line out of Peebles. There are also steeper walks with plenty of literary and historical interest which set out from Peebles, Traquair, Cardrona, Innerleithen and Clovenfords. A little further off the beaten track is a gem of a walk to an idyllic little loch sheltered by the hills south of Traquair.

Neidpath Castle ▸

Upper Tweed Valley

West Linton and the old roads

Distance 10km **Time** 2 hours 30
Terrain good tracks and paths, minor
road; take care on the woodland catwalk
Map OS Explorer 344 **Access** regular buses
from Edinburgh to West Linton

West Linton is situated at the point
where the Lyne Water, a tributary of the
Tweed, emerges from the Pentland Hills
and at the crossing of two ancient routes
across Lowland Scotland. When the
droving trade was at its height the village
hosted one of the largest sheep fairs in
Scotland. This walk into the hills follows
ancient highways and returns by a minor
road and a woodland catwalk.

From the Gordon Arms Hotel in West
Linton, cross over the A702 and head up
The Loan to the right of the Manor
Garage. Follow this stony track past some
grand houses to reach the old Roman
road which linked West Linton and
Carlops with Musselburgh and the east
coast. Follow the signpost, bearing right
for Carlops, until you reach the Siller
Holes just beyond a marshy pond. The
uneven ground on the flank of Lead Law
is where lead was once mined and
smelted, much of it for use in the
building and maintenance of the Borders
Abbeys; silver (siller) was also extracted
from the ground here.

Take the next sharp left to go past the
sheds of Stonypath Farm (closing all gates
behind you as you go) and carry on along
a good track which winds around the

WEST LINTON AND THE OLD ROADS

flank of Faw Mount. Look out for the little bridges over the burns flowing off the hillside and down to the Lyne Water on this section; evidence that this was once a very important route through the hills for drovers leading their livestock south from the markets at Crieff and Falkirk through the Pentlands to their final destination in England.

When you reach a drystane dyke, just past a big bend in the watercourse below, go left and shadow the wall down to the river (ignore the shoogly duckboards). Follow the infant river upstream to reach a wooden footbridge; cross over here and head up to the tarmac access road for Baddinsgill Reservoir.

Unless you want to extend the walk by taking a look at the reservoir, follow this open road back down towards West Linton before turning left at the sign for Lynedale House. Drop down to cross the river by the stone bridge and, on the other side, just after the pig enclosure, turn right into the rhododendron bushes and woodland.

Go through the gate to access the mixed woodland of Catwalk Den, home to pipistrelle bats, roe deer and foxes and managed by the Woodland Trust. Enjoy a precipitous view of the Lyne Water as you wind your way back along the narrow path to the busy A702 and the start.

◀ Footbridge over the Lyne Water

Broughton Heights

Distance 9km **Time** 2 hours 30 (out and back) **Terrain** good hill tracks and paths **Map** OS Explorer 336 **Access** regular Biggar to Peebles bus service stops in Broughton 1km from the start (except Sundays)

The young John Buchan spent his summer holidays at his sheep-farming grandparents' home in the Tweeddale village of Broughton. This route follows part of the path from the village to Peebles named after the prolific novelist, historian, war correspondent and statesman, before heading up to the highest point on the ridge of rounded hills to the north known as the Broughton Heights.

The walkers' car park at the start of the John Buchan Way is found by following the farm road signposted for Broughton Place off the A701 at the north end of Broughton. Follow the farm road through an impressive set of gateposts and past Broughton Place, a Scottish Baronial-style house designed by Sir Basil Spence, to reach the parking area by the side of a shepherd's cottage.

Go through the gate and follow the wide grassy track past the cottage and small woodland before dropping down to cross Hollows Burn. It is not hard to imagine a young Buchan leaping across here and heading off to explore the hills or to picture his dashing spy-catching hero of *The Thirty-Nine Steps*, Richard Hannay, looking out over the 'constantly changing prospect of brown hills and far green meadows', while enjoying the

◀ On the way to the Broughton Heights

'continual sound of larks and curlews and falling streams'.

Carry on along the track, with Clover Law on one side and Trahenna Hill and Hammer Head on the other, until you reach a split in the path with the John Buchan Way continuing to your right. Instead of following this down to Stobo and then on to Peebles, head left and make for the fence between Clover Law and Broomy Side.

Go over the stile by the gate and follow the fenceline along the exposed ridge over Green Law to reach the trig pillar on Pyked Stane Hill, the highest point on the Broughton Heights at 571m. On the way along the ridge look out for paragliders below – the hillside here is ideal for the sport.

From the summit there are great views on a clear day over Lanarkshire and the Pentland Hills to the north with the rounded Tinto prominent to the west beyond Biggar. The easiest option from the top is to retrace your steps and make your way back down through the glen to the start. To stay higher for longer, however, you could take the narrow path to your right just after you recross the stile and follow the fenceline along Clover Law's often boggy summit ridge before dropping down to rejoin the outward path near the shepherd's cottage.

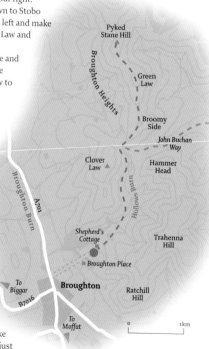

Neidpath Castle and the Tweed Walk

Distance **11km** Time **3 hours 30**
Terrain **mostly good paths, old railway bed
and minor roads** Maps **OS Explorer 336
and 337** Access **regular bus service from
Edinburgh and Galashiels stops in Peebles**

This walk passes Neidpath Castle,
a partly-ruined 14th-century towerhouse
which watches over the Tweed west of
Peebles, to follow the old Symington,
Biggar and Broughton Railway Line to
Lyne Station. The return takes in another
striking fortified tower at Barns, the
setting for John Buchan's *John Burnet of
Barns*, a historical romance portraying the
lives of Covenanters in the 17th century.

From Peebles' busy main street, head
towards the Tweed Bridge and turn right

just before it to pass the town's
swimming pool. Join the riverside path
into Hay Lodge Park and carry on along
the Tweed. Apart from an early diversion
up some steps and through a hole in a
wall, and some slippery rougher sections,
the signposted 'Tweed Walk' route is easy
to follow through the wooded valley.

Before long, Neidpath Castle comes into
view, perched on a crag high above the
Tweed. The path carries on to the unusual
skew-arch Neidpath Viaduct and – a little
further on – Manor Bridge. Don't be
tempted to cross the Tweed here; instead
cross over the road and go up the steps to
join the old railway track which closed in
the 1950s. Enjoy the open views and the
wildflowers which have reclaimed this

route as you stroll along it to Lyne Station.

When the railway bed runs out, cross over the Lyne and, once past some houses, take the path which leads to a footbridge over the Tweed. On the other side, turn left through woodland and follow the driveway to Barns Tower. Now painted a nice shade of pink, this typical 16th-century Borders house was recently restored and is now a romantic holiday let. Nearby, beside the Tweed, is the Georgian Barns House, dating to 1773.

From the tower, carry on until you reach a signpost directing you off the road and back to the Tweed. Take this pleasant path to follow the river downstream to Manor Bridge which you passed earlier. Again, don't cross this bridge; instead go up the steps and turn right to cross over the

Manor Water, a tributary of the Tweed, by the Old Manor Brig.

There is now a short steep climb up the brae at Manor Sware; it is worth the effort for the wonderful view back down over the Tweed. When you reach the car park and viewpoint, look for an opening on the other side of the road into South Park Wood. Follow the main path to the right down through the woodland, soon glimpsing Neidpath Castle through the trees. Once you have found the riverside path, make your way back past the castle and cross the Tweed by the Fotheringham Bridge to return to the start.

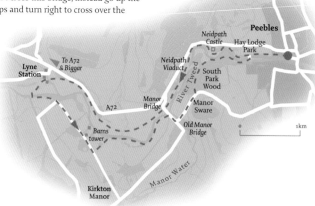

◀ Manor Bridge over the Tweed

Cademuir Hill and Manor Water

Distance 12km **Time** 3 hours 30
Terrain pavement, hillpaths and minor
road **Map** OS Explorer 337 **Access** regular
bus service from Edinburgh and Galashiels
stops in Peebles

On Cademuir Hill was one of John Buchan's
first published short stories and this walk
explores some of the hill country which
inspired him. The route initially follows
the John Buchan Way from Peebles to
Broughton before diverting to take in the
remains of the Iron Age forts on the
highest points of this sprawling hill.

The John Buchan Way starts from the
Kingsmeadows car park (no charge), just
over the Tweed from Peebles town centre.
Look for the John Buchan Way signage
which leads you along Caledonian Road,
opposite the car park entrance, and up a

vennel. Carry on up the lanes and turn
right after you have passed the school
playing fields. At the next junction, turn
left onto Edderston Road and go through
a metal gate on your right which leads
into a field. Follow the path by the stone
wall to reach another gate and then keep
with the waymarked route as it winds
through a gap in the hills.

John Buchan spent his childhood
holidays walking these hills and his first
collection of short stories, inspired by the
landscape and people of this area, was
published when he was just 21. Buchan
went on to produce over 30 novels, seven
short story collections and almost 100
works of non-fiction, as well as finding
time to serve as Lord High Commissioner
to the General Assembly of the Church
of Scotland and as Governor-General
of Canada.

Good views of Peeblesshire's rolling
hills begin to open up as you head
towards a dip in the ridge. There are

various other tempting paths, but don't leave the waymarked route until it starts to descend to the road. At this point bear right on the obvious path to visit the first of the forts.

Protected by steep slopes to the south, around 40 roundhouses were enclosed here by a massive perimeter wall, much of which has now fallen down the hillside. It is thought the fort was abandoned around 80AD as the Roman army advanced north. Further along the ridge, the second, and probably earlier, fort is smaller but you can clearly see how thick its walls were; look out too for the *chevaux de frise* – pointy stones half-buried in a gully to hamper any attack.

After exploring the forts, drop down to the road below and follow it to cross the Manor Water by an iron bridge. Bear right on the other side for Kirkton Manor and carry on until you reach the Manor Bridge over the Tweed. Cross over and take the riverside path all the way past Neidpath Castle to the swimming pool by the side of the Tweed Bridge. Cross over the bridge to return to the car park and the start.

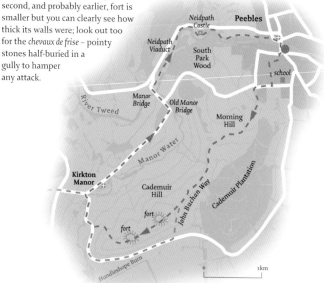

◀ Walkers on Cademuir Hill

Cardrona Forest and Tower

Distance **7km** Time **2 hours 30**
Terrain **woodland paths, sometimes
boggy, and plantation roads**
Map OS Explorer 337 Access **regular bus
service between Edinburgh and Galashiels
stops at Cardrona**

Cardrona Forest and the modern planned
village of Cardrona lie on the south bank
of the Tweed, midway between Peebles
and Innerleithen. This straightforward
circular walk through a variety of
managed woodlands visits the site
of an Iron Age hillfort and a ruined
16th-century towerhouse.

Start from the Forestry Commission car
park at Kirkburn on the back road from
Peebles to Traquair (B7062) and follow the
red 'Wallace's Trail' waymarkers past the
toilet block, heading south alongside the
Kirk Burn. After approximately 2km take a

sharp left, still following the red
waymarkers, up and around the north
flank of Wallace's Hill.

The trail winds through the trees and
crosses over forest roads before turning
north and rising steeply to reach the top
of Castle Knowe. The 19th-century
drystone sheepfold at the summit
obscures the fact that this was the site of
a major Iron Age fort which once held a
commanding position over a large stretch
of the Tweed Valley. The recycled stone
walls are also a reminder that more
recently this was all open hillside, grazed
by sheep, before the larch, spruce, pine
and fir plantations took over.

Keep with the red markers to drop down
to a forest road and follow this along as it
runs parallel with the busy A72. Keep a
good lookout as you walk along the road
for an informal path heading off on the

◀ The ruin of Cardrona Tower

right down the hillside: this goes past Cardrona Tower, the ruined and inaccessible 16th-century former stronghold of the Govan family. Towerhouses such as this are dotted all along the Tweed Valley and were built when violent cross-Border raids were commonplace. The Govans sold the tower to the Williamson family after falling into debt and the building was eventually abandoned when they built the more comfortable Cardrona House on lower ground nearby.

The tower's dark and damp basement is a haven for bats and is regularly monitored by Bat Conservation Trust volunteers, but it's best to pay attention to the signs and not get too close as some of the stonework is dangerously loose.

Rather than return to the forest road, stay with the path and make your way down the hillside and past the driveway of an impressive eco-mansion built into the fringe of the plantation. Follow the road back up to rejoin Wallace's Trail at the crossroads.

Enjoy the views over the Tweed Valley and keep with the forest road as it makes its way around the edge of the plantation before branching right to follow the red waymarkers down through a mixed woodland. Watch your footing on the steep path as you return to the start via the footbridge over the Kirk Burn.

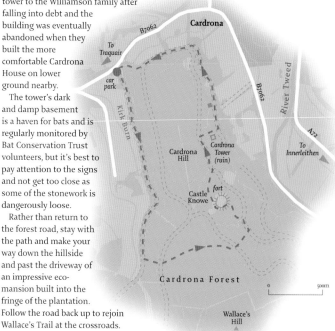

Lee Pen

Distance 5.5km **Time** 2 hours (out and back) **Terrain** woodland and hillpaths **Map** OS Explorer 337 **Access** regular bus service between Edinburgh and Galashiels stops in Innerleithen

This straightforward route up the distinctive peak of Lee Pen above Innerleithen is a great little hillwalk which can easily be extended for a longer day out.

Founded in 737AD by the pilgrim monk St Ronan, who is said to have sailed up the Tweed in a coracle and brought Christian teachings to these heathen parts, the bustling town of Innerleithen is situated on the banks of the Leithen Water at the base of the Moorfoot Hills.

Textile mills brought prosperity to the town in the 19th century and Sir Walter

Scott made it popular as a Victorian spa resort with his only contemporary novel *St Ronan's Well*, set in a thinly disguised Innerleithen. The sulphurous springs which Sir Walter enjoyed visiting as a boy still flow and the handsome sky-blue and white spa pavilion on Well Brae is well worth a visit.

To begin the walk turn off the main road through town at St Ronan's Terrace, directly opposite the Co-op. Continue through the wooden gate and up the tarmac access road for the radio mast on Caerlee Hill. The road steepens until you arrive at a bench on the crest of the ridge between Caerlee and Lee Pen.

Go right and head up the hill on the good path bordered by gorse bushes and a dyke. The way ahead along the ridge is obvious as the walking becomes easier

◄ Lee Pen from the Minchmoor Road

and a great view over the Tweed Valley opens up. Once past a plantation the path steepens again as you begin the last push for the stony summit.

At 502m, the summit is a great spot from which to survey the rolling Moorfoot Hills to the north and the course of the Tweed to the south with Minch Moor, another great viewpoint, to the southeast.

From here you can simply go back down the way you came up, or for a longer day out, carry on along the ridge to the top of Black Knowe before dropping down to the Leithen Water and returning to town.

Other attractions in and around Innerleithen include Robert Smail's Printing Works, which still uses old-fashioned printing methods on antique machines, and Traquair House, reputedly the oldest inhabited country house in Scotland and home to an excellent small brewery.

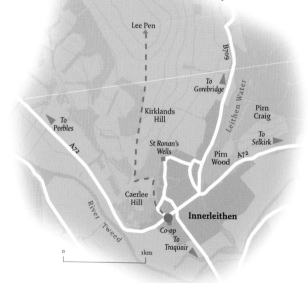

Lee Burn Head

Lee Pen

B709

To Gorebridge

Leithen Water

Kirklands Hill

Pirn Craig

To Peebles

A72

St Ronan's Wells

To Selkirk

Pirn Wood

A72

Caerlee Hill

River Tweed

Innerleithen

Co-op
To Traquair

0   1km

Minch Moor and the Cheese Well

Distance 8km **Time** 3 hours (out and back) **Terrain** good tracks and paths **Map** OS Explorer 337 **Access** no public transport to the start; Traquair is 3km from Innerleithen which has a regular bus service from Edinburgh and Galashiels

One of the oldest hillpaths in Scotland, the Minchmoor Road links the Yarrow and Tweed Valleys and was established by monks from Kelso visiting their lands in Lanarkshire. This straightforward walk takes in the summit of the hill which gives its name to the ancient route.

Start from the village hall in Traquair which can be found up the 'no through road' opposite the war memorial at the crossroads of the B7062 and B709. The route to the summit of Minch Moor is also part of the long-distance Southern Upland Way footpath, so from the car park follow the SUW marker up the road, past some houses and continue to a hard track bounded on both sides by a stone dyke.

Before long the views back over the Tweed Valley start to open up and a rather forlorn timber bothy is reached. Further on up the hill, cross the forestry roads and keep with the SUW posts as you follow the path through an area of cleared forestry.

When you reach Pipers Knowe you will see the *Point of Resolution* artwork. The 'growing sculpture' features a series of huge ovals cut into the heather which appear to change shape depending on your viewpoint.

A little further on and you come to the Cheese Well, an open spring marked by two stones into which travellers traditionally drop pieces of cheese to placate the local 'little people'.

As well as the Kelso monks, this route has been tramped by the Marquis of Montrose's weary soldiers retreating from the Battle of Philiphaugh and by the invading army of Edward I. More recently, Highland drovers herded their black cattle along it to Hawick and markets further south, no doubt stopping to leave something for the fairies to ensure a good price.

Carry on along the track until you reach a fingerpost which points south to the summit of Minch Moor (567m). Follow this to enjoy superb views of the Moffat, Manor and Moorfoot Hills as well as of the distinctive Eildons above Melrose. The summit area is also the high point of a challenging mountain biking route and you are more than likely to meet a rider or two preparing for their descent.

It is possible to get back to the forestry road passed earlier by one of the twisting tracks shared with ascending mountain bikers, but to enjoy the best views it is recommended that you turn around and return the way you came.

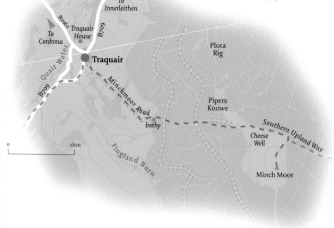

◀ Southern Upland Way artwork

Loch Eddy and the Glen

Distance 8km **Time** 3 hours **Terrain** estate roads and field paths **Map** OS Explorer 337 **Access** no public transport to the start

Tucked away in the valley of the Quair Water, 3km southwest of Traquair, the Glen Estate is the destination for this enjoyable walk to a picturesque and secluded loch once frequented by Prime Ministers and princesses.

Glen House is signposted off the minor road (B709) which links the Yarrow and Tweed Valleys. There is limited parking opposite the lodgehouse by the gate of the private drive to Glen House. Start the walk by following the estate road to the right rather than the private driveway and pass the rear of Glen House, several estate houses and an old red phonebox, before crossing the bridge over the Quair.

Glen House was commissioned by the industrialist Sir Charles Tennant and completed in 1855, but it was his grandfather, also Charles, who established the Tennant business dynasty by patenting bleaching powder in 1799. The ninth of 16 children born to an Ayrshire farming family, he went on to build the largest chemical works in the world at St Rollox in Glasgow and founded several businesses which eventually became Imperial Chemical Industries, or ICI. His success also allowed many of his descendants to marry into the English aristocracy and his grandson to become a baronet.

Carry on to pass the Glen Estate's village hall and various farm buildings before turning right and going through a gate by the farmhouse. Follow the 'high road' ahead through farmland, looking out for Loch Eddy set in the gully of Glendean

Banks away across the glen. The track eventually leads to a shepherd's cottage at the secluded and atmospheric Glenshiel Banks.

Pass the cottage and an old ruined dwelling and go through the wooden gate up ahead. Turn left on the rough path to shadow Gumscleuch Burn down over rough ground and reach the wooden boathouse by lovely Loch Eddy at the foot of Glendean Banks. The little man-made feeder loch for Glen House is thought to have been named after Charles Tennant's grandson, Edward Wyndham Tennant. Also known as Bim, he was a promising poet killed by a sniper's bullet on the Somme, aged just 19.

On a warm summer's day it is a lovely place to spend time and it's no surprise that the well-connected Tennants were fond of entertaining guests here; Prime Minister H H Asquith was among the many distinguished visitors

to this idyll, as was the very sociable Princess Margaret. It is possible to walk around the loch, but the path is narrow and exposed in places, so you may prefer just to head back down the glen to the farm on the 'low road'.

On the way, look out for a temple folly by the side of the road, now a memorial to two sons of the flamboyant Colin Tennant, the 3rd Baron Glenconner, who spent much of his inheritance turning the parched Caribbean island of Mustique into a playground for the 1970s jetset.

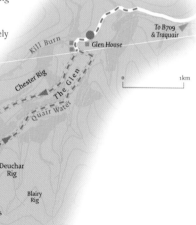

Meigle Hill

Distance 10km **Time** 3 hours 30
Terrain good tracks and open hillside
Map OS Explorer 338 **Access** regular bus
service from Edinburgh to Galashiels
stops at Clovenfords; trains from
Edinburgh to Galashiels

Meigle Hill lies between the River Tweed
and the Gala Water, just west of
Galashiels, and is easily accessed on a
network of popular paths. The summit
may be home to a collection of unsightly
towers and masts, but it sits apart from
other hills in the area and the views on
the way to the top are excellent.

Start from the Country Inn in
Clovenfords and follow Sir Walter Scott's
gaze across the roundabout and back
down the A72. Turn left along Caddonfoot
Road and look for the path leading off
into the woodland above the road.
Known locally as the Green Road or
the Velvet Path, this old coach road

shadows the A707 down the Caddon
gorge to Caddonfoot.

Carry on along the track to the
kirkyard just south of Caddonfoot and
turn left up the tree-sheltered side of
Blakehope Burn. Continue until you meet
a drystane dyke which rises up the
hillside. With the summit cairn of
Neidpath Hill directly behind you on the
other side of the valley, follow the wall all
the way up to an area of cleared forestry.
Make your way around to pick up the well-
made access road to the summit masts
and transmitters.

A large, rounded summit cairn is found
on the other side of the dyke in the
shelter of the trees. Nearby sits Wallace's
Putting Stone, a large erratic left behind
in the last ice age and said to have been
hurled at the English by the belligerent
patriot. William Wallace is a popular figure
in the Borders; The Kirk o' the Forest,
where he was reputedly proclaimed

◄ The Inn at Clovenfords

Guardian of Scotland in 1298, is not far away in Selkirk.

Carry on alongside the dyke and the trees and make your way down to a pumping station at the end of an access track. A wonderful view of Galashiels, the Eildon Hills and the distant Cheviots appears as you descend the hillside to meet the track.

Follow the track and turn left at the next junction to go around the top of a quarry popular with scrambling motorcyclists. On the other side of the A72, directly north, lie the remains of Torwoodlee Tower, built in 1601 by George

Pringle and still in the ownership of the family who founded Scotland's most famous knitwear brand.

The path continues across a couple of fields and runs parallel with the A72 below. In the area between the path and the road are the Meigle Pots, natural hollows which once hosted outlawed Covenanter field meetings in the 1640s.

At the next junction, above Meigle Farm, go left and then leave the access track and follow the signposted path back to the Green Road.

Turn right on the Green Road to return to Clovenfords.

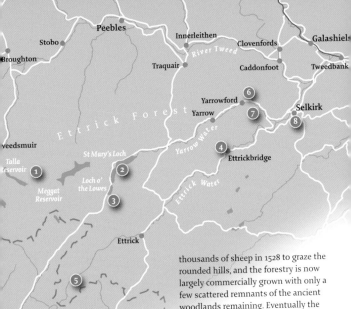

On a modern OS map 'Ettrick Forest' is squeezed between the Ettrick and Yarrow Waters and stretched out over an area where few trees stand. There is little to suggest that this was once a vast and wild mix of pine, oak, birch and hazel trees which provided shelter for lawless Border Reivers as well as countless deer and boar.

Kings of Scotland kept it as their personal hunting ground and both William Wallace and Robert the Bruce used the forest as their base during the Wars of Independence. Having had his sport, however, James V turned out thousands of sheep in 1528 to graze the rounded hills, and the forestry is now largely commercially grown with only a few scattered remnants of the ancient woodlands remaining. Eventually the Scotts of Buccleuch came to own much of the Ettrick Forest and the present Duke of Buccleuch, now the largest private landowner in the UK, still lives in Bowhill House, just west of Selkirk.

The walks in this section include high hill routes accessed from remote spots above the Megget Reservoir and down in the Ettrick Valley, as well as easier lochside rambles near Selkirk and at St Mary's Loch and the Loch of the Lowes on the road from Selkirk to Moffat. The Duke of Buccleuch's Bowhill Estate is the location of a wonderful carriage drive and not far away, on the other side of the Yarrow, is an enjoyable walk to a well-known hilltop meeting place marked by three cairns.

St Mary's Kirkyard and Loch ▶

Ettrick and Yarrow

Broad Law from the Megget Stane

Distance 9km **Time** 2 hours 30 (out and back) **Terrain** open hillside with faint paths; some boggy patches
Map OS Explorer 330 **Access** no public transport to the start

Broad Law is the highest hill in the Borders and the second highest in Southern Scotland (just 3m shorter than Galloway's mighty Merrick). This straightforward route starts high above the Talla and Megget Reservoirs in Tweeddale, making Broad Law one of the easier Corbetts (Scottish hills between 2500 and 3000ft high) to tick off your list if you have one.

This out and back route starts from the Megget Stane which marks an old 'trysting' or meeting place for travellers and drovers at the highest point of the pass linking St Mary's Loch and Tweedsmuir. The simple dressed stone is no towering megalith, however, and is easy to miss next to the cattle grid.

There is space for one car next to the cattle grid, but if it is taken there is a larger parking area not far along the road by the stone bridge which crosses the Talla Water just before it cascades down to the reservoir. Look out for cyclists making the torturous journey up from the farm at Linnfoots. This steep stretch of tarmac is also known as the 'Wall of Talla', one of the most notorious cycle hill climbs in the country.

From the cattle grid, head steeply up the spur of Fans Law, keeping on the east side of the old fence. The gradient eases off as you make your way on to Cairn Law and a number of shepherds' marker cairns soon come into view to the left and right of the vague path which continues to follow the line of the old fence.

The hard work for the day is almost over as you pass between the two most prominent cairns and views of the Megget Reservoir and St Mary's Loch open up to the east.

From Cairn Law the last 2km stretch is an enjoyable uphill stroll over (mostly) firm ground with a panoramic view over the rolling hill ranges of Southern Scotland to enjoy on a clear day.

Broad Law's summit is marked by a trig point, although the much more obtrusive construction is the nearby VOR (VHF Omni Directional Radio Range) station. This sends out a signal which enables aircraft on their way to Edinburgh Airport to stay on course, although advances in GPS technology are gradually making beacons of this type redundant. There is

also a police radio mast a short distance away to the northeast.

You can return by the same route or extend this walk to make a full day by carrying on to Dollar Law and going down by the path above the Cramalt Burn. This brings you down to the Megget Reservoir and a walk back up the road to the cattle grid.

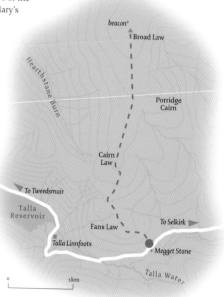

◄ The Megget Stane

Ring of St Mary's Loch

Distance 11km **Time** 3 hours
Terrain good hill and lochside paths;
sections of roadside verge
Maps OS Explorer 330 and 337
Access the Hawick Harrier service stops at
the Glen Café on Tuesdays and Thursdays
from July to the end of September

This signposted circular walk around the
largest natural loch in the Borders initially
follows the Southern Upland Way along
the peaceful east bank and through the
remnants of a former royal hunting forest
before joining an old drovers' path to
return to the start.

Start from Tibbie Shiel's Inn, a former
coaching house which sits on the neck of
land between St Mary's and her sister loch,
the Loch of the Lowes, just off the A708
Selkirk to Moffat road. There is ample free
parking opposite the roadside Glen Café, a
popular stop for bikers and cyclists. (The
walk can be done in either direction and

there is an alternative start point from the
car park at the north end of the loch.)

Above the road near the café is a
striking white monument to Ettrick-born
poet and novelist James Hogg who
enjoyed many evenings by the fire in the
inn which his statue now watches over.

Follow the minor road which heads
away from the A708 to reach the entrance
to the inn and look for the Ring of the
Loch and Southern Upland Way signposts.
Pass by the sailors' clubhouse and go
over the stiles as you follow the shoreline
path along.

All the hillsides around St Mary's
were once covered in pine, oak, birch and
hazel trees and the wild boar and deer
which lived here provided sport for
Scottish kings and their favoured
followers. The March Wood on the flank
of Bowerhope Law contains some of
the last remnants of the great forest
which was rapidly diminished with the

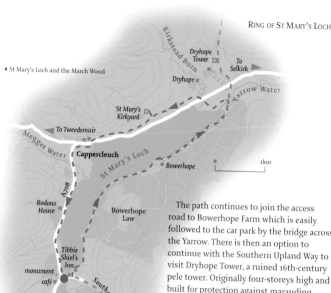

◀ St Mary's Loch and the March Wood

The path continues to join the access road to Bowerhope Farm which is easily followed to the car park by the bridge across the Yarrow. There is then an option to continue with the Southern Upland Way to visit Dryhope Tower, a ruined 16th-century pele tower. Originally four-storeys high and built for protection against marauding Reivers by ancestors of Sir Walter Scott, you can access the roofless top floor by a winding internal metal staircase for a good view over the loch.

Carry on to cross over the A708 and take the signposted path above the road. (Rejoin the walk here if you detoured to visit Dryhope Tower.) Following the course of an old drove road, the path continues beneath the atmospheric St Mary's Kirkyard, just a short detour up the hillside, before returning to the road at Cappercleuch.

At the junction with the road to the Megget Reservoir there is another optional detour to the Dow Linn waterfall. The last stage of the walk back to Tibbie's makes use of the wide roadside verge for short-lived sections where it is not possible to follow the shore.

introduction by James V of thousands of sapling-munching Cheviot sheep.

Across the loch from the March Wood you can see the impressive Rodono House, formerly an exclusive hotel famed for hosting wild society parties. A Model T Ford car is said to lie at the bottom of the loch in front of the house after it was driven onto the frozen water by one group of pranksters and left there as the ice melted. A harried Mandy Rice-Davies also took refuge here at the height of the Profumo scandal in the early 1960s.

Loch of the Lowes and Riskinhope Hope

Distance 10km **Time** 2 hours 30
Terrain mostly on hard tracks and clear paths, some bog-hopping on descent and by the loch **Map** OS Explorer 330
Access the Hawick Harrier service stops at the Glen Café on Tuesdays and Thursdays from July to the end of September

This undulating circular walk follows an old drove road up into the rounded hills above the Loch of the Lowes before returning by a lochside path. Much of the route is signposted as part of the coast to coast Southern Upland Way.

From the grassy car park opposite the Glen Café, just off the A708 Selkirk to Moffat road, walk south over the stone bridge and past the entrance to Tibbie Shiel's Inn. Pass Crosscleuch Farm and continue up the well-made Captain's Road, an old drover's route which winds over the hills to Tushielaw and Ettrick. Carry on to reach the gate at Berrybush Forest. Leave the Captain's Road here and follow the Southern Upland Way marker post to the right.

Cross over Crosscleuch Burn by the footbridge and follow the path as it skirts around Earl's Hill. Stick with the Southern Upland Way markers (don't rejoin the signposted Captain's Road) and cross another footbridge just before you

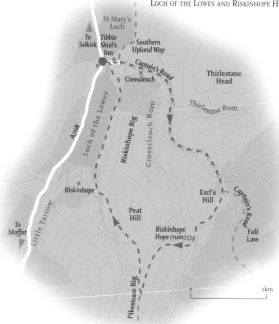

reach the ruin at Riskinhope Hope.

'Hope' means 'a sheltered valley', so this doubly sheltered spot is a good place to take a rest, admire the sheep buchts on the hillside opposite and contemplate the life of the shepherd and his family who once lived here.

Still looking out for Southern Upland Way marker posts, leave Riskinhope Hope behind and climb steadily up onto the spur of Pikestone Rig. Keep on along the broad grassy track until you reach two marker posts close together. Leave the Southern Upland Way here, just before it

starts to drop down to the Ettrick Valley, and take the path to the right down the hillside towards the Loch of the Lowes; although boggy and indistinct in places at first, the track improves as it goes around the flank of Peat Hill and the Loch of the Lowes comes into view.

As you approach the buildings of Riskinhope Farm, bear right and go through a field gate. Follow the edge of the field to reach a second gate and head towards the loch. From here, you can pick up the lochside path which leads back to the car park off the A708.

Kirkhope Tower and Hill

Distance 6km **Time** 1 hour 30
Terrain hill paths, sometimes vague with
boggy sections **Map** OS Explorer 337
Access limited bus service from Selkirk
and Hawick to Ettrick

Kirkhope Tower sits at the foot of
Kirkhope Hill looking over the pretty
village of Ettrickbridge, 10km southwest
of Selkirk. This adventurous short walk
leads you past the 16th-century tower and
up to a windswept summit with views
over the tranquil Ettrick Valley.

From Kirkhope Kirk (parking by the
railings) in Ettrickbridge, go past the
school and follow Woodend Road to its
end, before turning right to go through a
gate and onto a farm track. Shortly after
passing a tin shed take the track on

your left up the hillside and join the path
which contours around to Tower Burn.

As the path fades, bear right and
drop down to cross the burn by a
wooden footbridge in the shadow of
Kirkhope Tower.

Kirkhope was abandoned in the mid-
19th century but rescued from ruin in the
1990s and restored as a private residence.
It was originally built by the Scotts of
Harden in the early 16th century and
destroyed by a party of marauding
Armstrongs in 1543 during the campaign
by Henry VIII of England to force the
marriage of his son Edward to Mary,
Queen of Scots, a conflict which came to
be known as 'The Rough Wooing'.

The tower was later rebuilt by the
notorious Reiver Walter Scott of Harden,

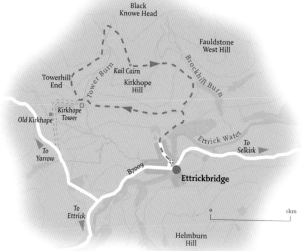

Black
Knowe Head

Fauldstone
West Hill

Tower Burn

Brockhill Burn

Kail Cairn

Towerhill
End

Kirkhope
Hill

Kirkhope
Tower

Old Kirkhope

Ettrick Water

To
Selkirk

To
Yarrow

B7009

Ettrickbridge

To
Ettrick

0   1km

Helmburn
Hill

or 'Auld Wat', whose wife famously presented him with his spurs on a platter whenever their stores were running low.

Wat's cattle-reiving raids, usually under cover of darkness in Northumbria, left a trail of destruction and often cost lives. He was not all bad, however. When a young hostage taken during a raid was accidentally drowned crossing the Ettrick, the remorseful Wat built a bridge to salve his conscience, and his coat-of-arms, with the family motto *Cornua Reparabit Phoebe*, 'There will be moonlight again', was carved in the stonework. The coat-of-arms was transferred to the present crossing in Ettrickbridge when the original collapsed in 1777. One of Auld Wat's direct descendants was Sir Walter Scott, novelist and poet.

Go through the gate beside the tower

and, on the other side of the parking area, head steeply up the craggy hillside of Towerhill End on a vague path. Make your way north to a sheepfold and, once on flatter, boggier ground, shadow the Tower Burn to reach a gate at the meeting of two electric fences. Go through the gate and keep above the watercourse, following a faint path, until you see another sheepfold at the head of the burn. Cross over the water and follow the sheep trods to reach the Kail Cairn on the summit ridge of Kirkhope Hill.

After enjoying the view, head east, using the distant and distinctive Eildon Hills near Melrose as your guide, before picking up a grassy track which will take you back down to the tin shed passed earlier on. From here return to Woodend Road and the start.

◄ Kirkhope Tower

Ettrick Pen

Distance **15km** Time **3 hours 30**
Terrain **forest roads and hill paths; boggy
in places** Map **OS Explorer 330**
Access **no public transport to the start**

**The Ettrick Horseshoe at the end of the
Ettrick Valley is a round of hills popular
with walkers looking to bag a handful of
'Donalds' – peaks over 2000ft. This route
follows the Southern Upland Way to join
the horseshoe halfway round at the
Borders regional boundary before tackling
Ettrick Pen, the highest of the hills. There
is a fair bit of ascent and exposure, so you
need to be properly prepared.**

Start the walk from the end of the
Ettrick Valley road; there is limited
parking by the side of the turning circle.
Take the forest access road towards the
old Potburn farmhouse and carry on over
the wooden bridge to reach the Over

Phawhope Bothy, a welcome refuge for
walkers on the Southern Upland Way
maintained by the Mountain Bothies
Association. At the signposted junction,
just beyond the bothy, ignore the track
marked for Ettrick Pen and follow the
SUW up into the forestry.

At the next SUW markerpost, leave the
forest road and make your way through
the last of the trees to reach the open
hillside. Carry on to the regional
boundary at Ettrick Head and turn
immediately left with the fence.
After making your way as best you can
around some fearsome peat hags, follow
the fenceline steeply up the flank of
Wind Fell.

Keep with the fence when you reach
the top of Wind Fell and carry on to craggy
Hopetoun Craig. Pass a variety of
shepherds' marker stones and cairns

◀ Ettrick Pen

erected over the years on the final push to the summit of Ettrick Pen. The word *Pen* derives from the Brittonic or Old Welsh language and means 'head' or 'hilltop' and the large scattered cairn here suggests that this was once an important site with a ceremonial or religious use.

To make your way back down to Phawhope Bothy, head west on a faint path with the distinctive peak of White Shank on the other side of the valley straight ahead. The path then trends left as it drops steeply down to the sheep fank above the Entertrona Burn. Pick up the farm track here and return to the bothy and the turning circle at Potburn.

On the way back through the Ettrick Valley look out for the roadside memorial to the poet and novelist James Hogg, also known as the Ettrick Shepherd, who was born in Ettrick and is buried in the churchyard. His most important work, *The Private Memoirs and Confessions of a Justified Sinner*, is considered one of the major Scottish novels and is cited as an influence by many modern writers, including Irvine Welsh and Ian Rankin.

Another notable local was Thomas Boston, a preacher and theologian who wrote several popular collections of sermons. He is remembered in the name of the red and white Boston Memorial Hall opposite the primary school.

57

Three Brethren from Yarrowford

Distance 12km Time 3 hours
Terrain good paths and hill tracks
Map OS Explorer 338 Access the Hawick
Harrier service on Tuesdays and Thursdays
from July to the end of September will stop
at Yarrowford on request

Constructed in the 16th century by local
lairds to mark their land boundaries, the
handsome trio of summit cairns known as
the Three Brethren are a popular Borders
walking destination. There is a choice of
routes to the top; this one begins at
Yarrowford with a short woodland walk to
reach the open hill.

Start from the parking area with the red
telephone box by the side of the A708 at
Yarrowford. Go down the road towards
Broadmeadows Bridge and turn up into
the modern houses on your left before the
bridge. A path leads off on the right, just
before the drive to Broadmeadows House,
which shadows the Yarrow and then Old
Broadmeadows Burn through woodland.

Carry on along the woodland path to
pass Broomy Law Cottage (formerly the
Broadmeadows Youth Hostel) on your left.
Soon after, you arrive at a gate which leads
onto open hillside. Once through the gate,
turn right with the wall and then follow
the track left as it heads steeply over the
saddle of Foulshiels Hill.

A now-ruined cottage at Foulshiels
at the foot of the hill was the birthplace
of Mungo Park, Victorian explorer and
pioneer of African studies. He died during

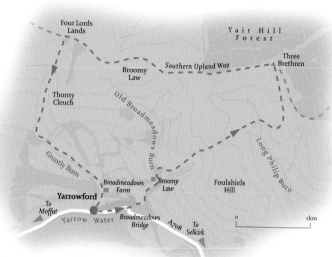

his second expedition to Africa in 1806 after being attacked by natives. In his memory the Mungo Park Medal is presented annually by the Royal Scottish Geographical Society and there is a statue of the explorer on Selkirk High Street.

After dropping down the hillside to cross over Long Philip Burn go through the gate and pick up any of the small paths that soon join with the wider track which comes up from Philiphaugh. The Three Brethren, visible on the crest of the hill, are straight ahead.

Once you have soaked up the views from the summit cairns, turn left and follow the Southern Upland Way on a good hard track with the Yair Hill Forest blanketing the hillside on your right. This is the Minchmoor Road, used by drovers for centuries to link the Yarrow and Tweed Valleys. Before you reach the saddle of Broomy Law a wooden stile over the wall leads to a path back down Old Broadmeadows Burn to the woodland you left earlier. To stay higher for longer, however, continue with the SUW around Broomy Law before reaching the dip in the ridge at Four Lords Lands. Leave the SUW here and pick up the path down the hillside which shadows the Cameron and then the Gruntly Burn all the way down to Broadmeadows Farm and then on to the parking area by the A708.

◀ The Three Brethren

The Duchess's Drive and Newark Castle

Distance 12km Time 3 hours
Terrain good waymarked tracks and estate
roads Maps OS Explorer 337 and 338
Access the Hawick Harrier service stops at
Bowhill on Tuesdays and Thursdays from
July to the end of September

The Duke of Buccleuch and Queensberry's
magnificent Bowhill House sits in the
valley of the Yarrow Water near Selkirk and
is the starting point for this enjoyable
waymarked moorland walk along a
Victorian carriage drive.

From the car park (seasonal parking
charge) behind Bowhill House, go left and
follow the estate road until you see a
marker post with a yellow arrow off to the
right, pointing the way into the forest.
Carry on through the plantation (unless
there is harvesting going on and diversion
signs in place) to pass a stone seat with the

initials BQ (Buccleuch and Queensberry).

A little further on the carriage drive
emerges from the forestry onto heather
moorland; look back to enjoy a view of
the three Eildon Hill summits as you rise
to meet the saddle between Fastheugh
and Fauldshope Hills. Look out too for
stone mile marker posts at the side of
the track.

Pass a line of well-built grouse butts as
the drive curves around the hillside and
rises to meet a gate. From here you can
follow a quad bike track, which becomes
more distinct as you climb, to take in the
summit of Fastheugh Hill, or continue
with the main drive around the side of the
hill. Either way, there are great views as the
Yarrow Valley opens below.

Keep with the yellow marker posts and
the carriage drive as you make your way
towards Newark Hill. The windblown

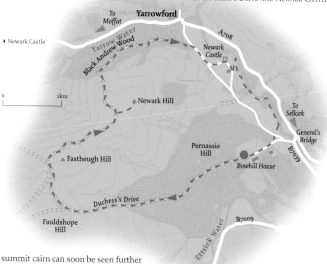

summit cairn can soon be seen further along the ridge to the right – the short detour out and back is worth it for the view over Bowhill House and gardens.

Back on the drive, drop down to meet a gate at the edge of Black Andrew Wood and follow the marker posts through the trees to a tarmac estate road and the end of the carriageway. Go right and follow the estate road before bearing left at the next junction to reach the sombre ruin of Newark Castle.

Built in 1423 by the Douglas family, the towerhouse was gifted to the wife of James III, Margaret of Denmark, in 1473. The royal arms can be seen on the west gable. There is some dark history attached to Newark; in 1645 at least 100 Irish foot soldiers from Manus O'Cahan's Regiment under the command of the Royalist Marquis of Montrose and many of their followers, including women and children, were executed by Sir David Leslie's Covenanters in the courtyard after being promised clemency in the aftermath of the Battle of Philiphaugh.

From the castle you can carry on along the road all the way back to the main drive. However, for a more interesting walk, turn sharply left at the first junction you come to down to the Yarrow and pick up the signposted riverside Lady's Walk. Enjoy the wildflowers and birdlife as you make your way back to the drive to Bowhill House.

The house and gardens (entry fee) are well worth exploring and there is a good café as well as a number of options for enjoyable shorter walks.

The Haining

Distance 2.5km Time 1 hour
Terrain good woodland paths with some
steps Map OS Explorer 338 Access regular
bus services from Edinburgh and Carlisle
to Selkirk

Sited on a terrace of hills overlooking the
Ettrick Water, Selkirk was once the capital
of a royal hunting forest full of wild boar
and herds of deer. The mansion house of
the Haining Estate, on the southern edge
of the town, dates from the 18th century
although *haining* is an old Scots word for
'enclosure' and deer were hunted here for
sport much earlier. This short walk around
the loch and woodland is one of the royal
burgh's hidden treasures.

Start from the car park by Halliwell's
House Museum and go through a gateway
in the wall to access The Haining Estate.
Follow the path to the left and go uphill
through an area of young trees, then cross

a track and go up some steps to enter a
more mature woodland on an often
muddy path.

The path soon drops down, crossing an
avenue of lime trees on the way to the
loch. Along the way, look out on your right
for the stepped terrace on which the
strategically important 12th-century motte-
and-bailey-style Selkirk Castle once stood.

A little further on you can enjoy a view of
the Palladian mansion house at the head
of the loch from a waterside viewing
platform off to the right. Built in the 1790s
by the Pringle family, the house was
requisitioned during the Second World War
and occupied by Polish soldiers. It is said
that after the war their redundant guns
and ammunition were thrown into the
deep waters of the loch. The house and
stables were bequeathed to the people of
Selkirkshire in 2009 by the last private
owner of the estate and are now managed

◀ Haining Loch

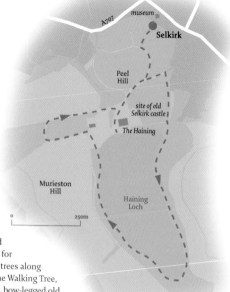

Selkirk

museum

A707

Peel
Hill

site of old
Selkirk castle

The Haining

Murieston
Hill

Haining
Loch

0   250m

by a charitable trust.

Carry on to enjoy a
pleasant walk around
the loch, looking out for
some impressive old trees along
the way, including The Walking Tree,
an unusually-shaped, bow-legged old
beech, off the main path on the west
side of the loch.

Soon after passing the derelict
boathouse you arrive at the old stable
block which now houses artists studios
and holiday apartments. West of the
stables are old bear and wolf enclosures in
which Captain John Pringle kept his
unusual pets in the 1820s. The famous
mascot of the Polish Free Army, Wojtek the
bear, is also said to have spent some time
here before enjoying his retirement from
service at Edinburgh Zoo.

Follow the waymarked path to the
left away from the stables and mansion

house and head up and along the edge
of a field with an old ruined dovecot in it.
Go right at the next junction and carry on
to meet the access road to the stable
block and mansion. You can continue
along here to complete the circuit or go
around the mansion to visit the lochside
terrace. A pair of Antonio Canova-inspired
busts by the edge of the water mark the
completion of extensive additions to the
estate in the 1820s.

Return to the front of the mansion and
follow the path back through the trees to
the car park.

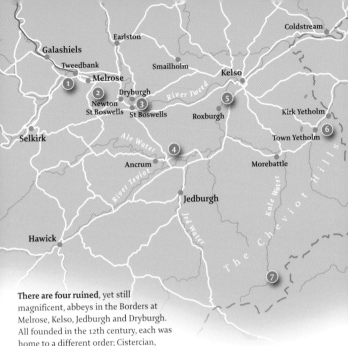

There are four ruined, yet still magnificent, abbeys in the Borders at Melrose, Kelso, Jedburgh and Dryburgh. All founded in the 12th century, each was home to a different order; Cistercian, Tironensian, Augustinian and Premonstratensian respectively. Given the turbulent history of the area it is remarkable that they survived for as long as they did, although all of them had to be rebuilt at regular intervals after being overrun by marauding armies.

The Borders Abbeys Way, a long-distance walking route which links the four great sites, is utilised on some of the routes in this chapter. The other divinely-inspired route through the Borders is the St Cuthbert's Way which links Melrose to Holy Island. The coast-to-coast Southern Upland Way also briefly features, as does

the cross-border Pennine Way which terminates in Kirk Yetholm. The route which pre-dates them all was built by the Romans, however, and Agricola's Road, or Dere Street as it was later known, is joined for a walk into the Cheviot Hills.

It is not surprising that so many long-distance routes criss-cross this part of the Borders; as well as the abbeys, the towns of Melrose, St Boswells, Kelso and Jedburgh are full of history and interest, and there are many great country estates, such as those at Harestanes and Abbotsford, which have long been welcoming to walkers.

Kelso Abbey ▶

Melrose, Kelso and Jedburgh

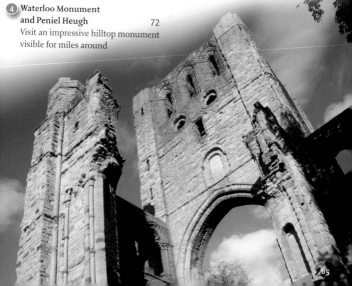

Abbotsford and Melrose

Distance 14.5km **Time** 4 hours
Terrain good hill tracks and paths,
railway bed and minor road
Map OS Explorer 338 **Access** regular bus
services link Melrose to Edinburgh, Kelso,
Jedburgh and Tweedbank Station

The bustling town of Melrose clusters
around the soaring pink sandstone ruins
of its Abbey which was founded in 1136
by Cictercian monks. This long and
varied walk explores the surrounding
countryside and visits Abbotsford, the
wonderful former home of Sir Walter
Scott, before returning to town along the
banks of the writer's beloved Tweed.

Leave Market Square in Melrose by
Dingleton Road and turn right to reach the
handsome old railway station. Make your
way up to the platform and turn right on
the route of the dismantled Waverley Line.
Continue all the way along to the
underpass under the A6091 which brings
you out at the Borders General Hospital.

Follow the road past the hospital
entrance and through farmland towards a
line of electricity pylons. Take the
signposted path here for Rhymer's Glen
and follow it up into the woodland. This
enchanting glen takes its name from the
tale of Thomas the Rhymer who was
spirited away by the Queen of Elfland and
returned with the gift of foresight.

At the top of the woods keep with the
path over an old hillfort to a gate onto
Bowen Moor. Stay with the wall to reach

the woodland on the north side of Cauldshiels Loch and wind your way down to the water, looking out for the loch's resident kelpie, or water-horse.

From the end of the loch follow the track signposted for the Borders Abbeys Way to the quiet back road and turn left. Just before the house at the end, turn right and follow the path down through woodland and farmland before crossing the B6360 and joining the riverside path along the south bank of the Tweed.

Go with the flow of the river to arrive in front of Abbotsford, Sir Walter Scott's neo-Baronial 'conundrum castle', a house stuffed full of treasures, relics and

curiosities from Scottish history and where the great man wrote all his best works. (Tickets to visit the house and gardens are available from the excellent visitor centre.)

To continue the walk after Abbotsford, return to the Tweed and go under the A6091 and then the Redbridge Viaduct, again following the Borders Abbeys Way. It is now a long looping riverside stroll back around Tweedbank to Melrose, following the markers for the Southern Upland Way. Keep with the Tweed until you see the Chain Bridge which links Melrose with Gattonside on the other side of the river. With the Eildon Hills straight ahead above Melrose, follow the road back past the abbey to the start.

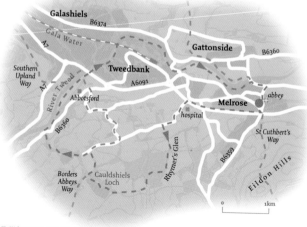

◀ Sir Walter Scott's Abbotsford

The Eildon Hills

Distance 9 to 12km (depending on how many of the three peaks you visit)
Time 3 to 4 hours Terrain good paths and tracks Map OS Explorer 338 Access regular bus services link Melrose to Edinburgh, Kelso, Jedburgh and Tweedbank Station

The Eildon Hills are a mini mountain range of three rounded tops, just south of Melrose, that have long been shrouded in mystery and legend. According to one tale, they were formerly one peak which was split into three on the orders of a wizard, and in another King Arthur and his knights lie asleep beneath them waiting for the day they will arise and ride again.

From Melrose Abbey, one of the four great Border Abbeys, go up Abbey Street, across Market Square and on past the Station Hotel on Dingleton Road. Walk under the bypass and look for the signposted steps between houses on the left. Go down them, then up a long flight of wooden steps which lead to a path between fields. Soon bustling Melrose is left far behind as you head up the hillside farmland. At the end of the path ignore all the dogwalkers' trails and bear right to reach the saddle between the two main summits.

At the tangled crossroads of paths on more level ground, choose which top to tackle first: Eildon Hill North is on your left, Eildon Mid Hill on your right and Eildon Wester Hill straight ahead, then right. All of them are worth the effort; although the Mid Hill, a favourite of Sir Walter Scott, is the highest at 422m (and has the steepest path to the top).

◄ Eildon Hill North

There is a good view of the Leaderfoot Viaduct over the Tweed from the summit of the North Hill and the remains of some 300 hut platforms, excavated from the solid bedrock to provide flat foundations for wooden roundhouses, can also be seen.

The hilltop was later developed by the Roman army under Agricola as a signal station, an important part of a large network of activity centred on Newstead, just east of Melrose, then called Trimontium (after these three peaks). The ditch which encircled the signal tower, probably the largest in Scotland, is still visible.

More fancifully, the Eildon Hills are where Scotland's very own Nostradamus, Thomas of Ercildoune, *aka* Thomas the Rhymer, met the Fairy Queen in a tale made popular by Sir Walter Scott. Carried off to Elfland under the Eildons by the queen, he returned with the gift of prophecy and the inability to tell a lie.

Once you have enjoyed all the diversions, leave the hills by branching off the St Cuthbert's Way path and heading down to the Eildon Hall woodland. In the trees, bear left, then follow the good track as it bends right and contours around the hillside, enjoying the call of nuthatches and great spotted woodpeckers as you go. At a signposted gate leave the woodland and cross farmland at the foot of the North Hill. You soon arrive at a tarmac road; go right, then left down a grassy track enclosed by hedges to the subway under the busy bypass.

Follow the path under the old railway and join the Borders Abbeys Way back along Priorswalk to the abbey and the start.

St Boswells and the Tweed

Distance 7.5km **Time** 2 hours 30
Terrain riverside paths and minor roads
Map OS Explorer 338 **Access** regular buses
from Edinburgh, Tweedbank and
Jedburgh stop in St Boswells

The stretch of the Tweed between
Mertoun Bridge and the suspension
footbridge at Dryburgh makes for one of
the finest riverside walks in the land,
particularly memorable when rich
autumn colours are reflected in the
flowing waters. The easy circular route
passes Dryburgh Abbey, burial place of
Sir Walter Scott, and a lovely place to
explore monastic life.

Start from St Boswells village green and
follow the Main Street up past the post
office and the award-winning Mainstreet
Trading bookshop and deli. Turn left up
Braeheads Road and then right to follow
the St Cuthbert's Way signposts down to
the golf course.

After the clubhouse, pick up the path
behind the trees which skirts the fairways
and greens and follow it down to the
riverbank. Ignore the weir across the Tweed
and stick with the path to reach the B6404
and Mertoun Bridge.

Once over the bridge (watch out for
fast-moving traffic) bear left and keep with
the Borders Abbeys Way signposts.

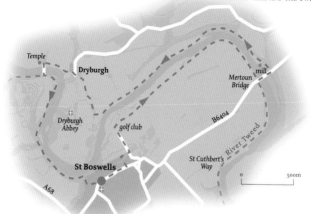

Continue to a split in the path and stay left along the field edge, then return to the riverbank as you head towards Dryburgh. Eventually the Borders Abbeys Way turns right, away from the Tweed, and passes a walled garden before it arrives at the visitors' car park of Dryburgh Abbey which sits in a loop of the river surrounded on three sides by water.

Founded in 1150 by white-robed Premonstratensian monks, originally from northern France, and then Alnwick in Northumberland, Dryburgh Abbey was often caught in the crossfire when Scotland and England fell out. In 1322 Edward II's defeated army burnt it down after hearing the bells within being rung to celebrate a Scottish victory. Despite this, and other disruptions, the monks managed to survive here until the Scottish Reformation.

From the abbey car park, carry on past the entrance to Dryburgh Abbey Hotel and keep left at the next junction. Follow the road to return to the riverside, passing an elaborate set of orchard gates erected by the Earl of Buchan in memory of his parents. A little further on you pass the old gardeners' cottages with a turreted tower named after the sculptor Edwin Stirling, a former resident.

Before crossing the suspension bridge look up on your right for the Temple of the Muses, a tribute to the Borders poet James Thomson (1700-1748) who wrote the words to the Victorian singalong *Rule, Britannia!*, as well as 'The Seasons', a series of four reflective nature poems which greatly influenced later Romantics.

Over the bridge, turn left and follow the signs for St Cuthbert's Way to rejoin the riverbank. After passing a fast-flowing stretch of the Tweed the path heads uphill by some steps to reach a road which is easily followed back to the village green.

◄ Fishing on the Tweed with the Eildons beyond

71

Waterloo Monument and Peniel Heugh

Distance **8km** Time **2 hours**
Terrain **good paths and country lanes**
Map **OS Explorer OL16** Access **the Jedburgh to Edinburgh bus will stop on request on the A68, west of Harestanes**

This part of the Borders is a long way from the battlefield in Belgium which the landmark 48m-high tower on top of Peniel Heugh, near Ancrum, commemorates. This walk is no epic struggle either, rather an easy circuit through pleasant woodland and along peaceful back roads.

From the car park of the excellent Harestanes Visitor Centre go between the craft courtyard and the children's play area to follow the path which runs parallel to the drive. Carry on to pass the old cricket field, following the red and green markers.

At a junction, go right towards Monteviot House and then turn left on the driveway and head up to the road. Cross directly over the B6400 and continue towards the gamekeeper's house, turning off on a path to the right before you reach it to go along the edge of the wood.

When you reach the back road, go right briefly along the road, then head left up a signposted track through the woodland. Soon you get your first view of the monument peeping over the top of the hill, but rather than jumping over the gate, stick with the main track for an easier approach. Before long you leave the woods behind for open hillside with the mighty monument up ahead.

Completed in 1824, nine years after the

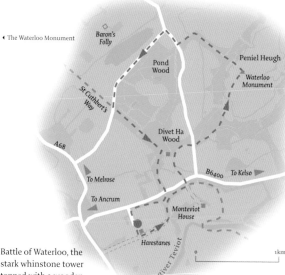

◄ The Waterloo Monument

Battle of Waterloo, the stark whinstone tower topped with a wooden pagoda was commissioned by William Kerr, 6th Marquis of Lothian, to celebrate the Duke of Wellington's decisive, though costly, victory over the ambitious Emperor Napoleon. It was a ferocious encounter in which 50,000 men are thought to have been slain in the space of just ten hours. Among them were many men from the Borders serving with the Royal North British Dragoons (The Scots Greys) who reputedly turned the battle by charging headlong into the French infantry lines crying out 'Scotland Forever!'. After seizing the prized Imperial Eagle battle standard, The Greys were thereafter known as 'the birdcatchers' within the British army.

To leave the hilltop, look for a stile on the edge of the woodland to the north of the monument and follow the path down through the trees to a barrier just before a minor road. Turn right and walk along the road, then go left at the next junction and carry on to pass Folly Loch on your right.

Look out for a gap in the wall at the side of the road waymarked with a Roman Helmet; this is Dere Street, the old Roman road and now part of St Cuthbert's Way, a 100km-long walking route from Melrose to Holy Island off the Northumbrian coast.

Follow the path through woodland back to the B6400, then go right at a footbridge to return to the visitor centre via the sawmill entrance.

Kelso to Roxburgh

Distance **10km** Time **3 hours**
Terrain **riverside path and old railway bed**
Map **OS Explorer 339** Access **regular bus
service from Edinburgh to Kelso**

This walk follows the River Teviot, one
of the main tributaries of the Tweed, to
reach a magnificent disused 14-arched
viaduct by the peaceful village of
Roxburgh, passing the site of a once
important Border stronghold on the way.

From Kelso Abbey, once the most
important of the Borders Abbeys, head
past the war memorial and cross Rennie's
Bridge over the Tweed. Turn right along
the A699 and follow it past the confluence
of the Teviot and the Tweed before
crossing another bridge over the Teviot.
On the far bank of the Tweed you will see
the wonderful Floors Castle, seat of the
Dukes of Roxburghe.

Go over a stone stile on your left soon
after the bridge and pick up the riverside
path which is also part of the Border
Abbeys Way linking Melrose, Dryburgh,
Jedburgh and Kelso. As you make your
way round the bend look up to your right
to spot the remains of Roxburgh Castle.

Overlooking the junction of the Teviot
and Tweed, this was once a key stronghold
that regularly changed hands between
Scotland and England. King James II of
Scotland was killed by an exploding
cannon during a siege here in 1460 and his
queen, Mary of Guelders, had the castle
demolished soon after capturing it.

Carry on along the river, enjoying the
open views of the surrounding
countryside and looking out for heron and
kingfisher, until you come to a stile which
takes you onto a minor road. Go along
here, through Roxburgh Mill Farm and

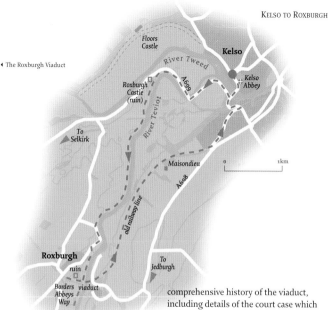

◄ The Roxburgh Viaduct

towards Roxburgh village, before taking the lane on your left to return to the riverside. Follow the river to reach the Grade A-listed viaduct which was built in 1850 as part of the St Boswells to Coldstream line.

You can cross the Teviot here by the delightful iron footbridge suspended on the side of the viaduct; however, if you go up the lane on your right just before you reach the viaduct, you will get a view of the ruins of a 16th-century towerhouse built by the Kerr family. At the top of the lane there is also a bus shelter by the side of the road which contains a comprehensive history of the viaduct, including details of the court case which followed the deaths of nine workers when an abutment collapsed.

To cross the Teviot, you can go back down the lane and over the suspension bridge or carry on past the bus shelter and follow the course of the railway back over the top of the viaduct; either way, you will soon be walking along the old hawthorn-lined railway bed towards Kelso.

Eventually you will see a striking white farmhouse up on your right – this is Maisondieu, formerly a medieval hospice. Just past here, the track becomes a woodland path which eventually leads to Jedburgh Road. Follow this to reach Station Road and turn left to return to Rennie's Bridge and the start.

Kirk Yetholm and Halterburn

Distance 10km **Time** 3 hours
Terrain hill paths, tracks and minor roads
Map OS Explorer OL16 **Access** regular
buses from Kelso to Town Yetholm and
Kirk Yetholm

The twin villages of Town Yetholm and
Kirk Yetholm lie on either side of the
Bowmont Water, close to the border with
England, and were home for a long time
to the 'royal house' of Scottish gypsies.
The last of the line, His Majesty King
Charles Faa Blythe, was crowned on Kirk
Yetholm's village green in 1898. This is
also the end of the line for walkers on the
Pennine Way which starts 429km away in
Edale, Derbyshire. This walk returns on
the trail after exploring some of the local
hills on a rolling ridge walk.

From the bus stop in Town Yetholm
head south along the B6401 and look out

for a colourful collection of gnomes on
your right as you leave town. A little
further on, turn left at the road to the
cemetery to cross the Bowmont Water at
Duncanhaugh Mill.

Follow the road around, past the farm
buildings at Hayhope, before turning left
up a grassy track. With Sunnyside Hill in
front of you, the track makes its way uphill
between Staerough Hill and Shereburgh.

As the track fades, cross a field between
gorse bushes on a vague path before
dropping down to a marshier area at the
foot of the rise to Sunnyside. After you
have negotiated your way around the
rough ground, the drystane dyke you see
up ahead can be shadowed all the way
over the hill. The view over the Cheviots
from the ridge is well worth the effort of
the steep pull to the top.

The dyke makes navigation easier on

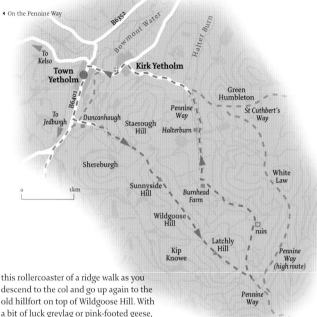

◀ On the Pennine Way

this rollercoaster of a ridge walk as you descend to the col and go up again to the old hillfort on top of Wildgoose Hill. With a bit of luck greylag or pink-footed geese, regular visitors to the area, will be flying overhead as you reach the summit.

Carry on in the same direction to take in Latchly Hill, the last climb of the day, before dropping down to meet up with the Pennine Way at Piper's Faulds. From here, rather than carrying on into England, turn left and head down the Halterburn Valley. The route is signposted all the way to Yetholm and visits the picturesque ruins of Old Halterburnhead, the only shelter on this last section of the Pennine Way, before bypassing the more modern Halterburnhead Farm.

Before long you are on a quiet tarmac road which gently climbs back to Kirk Yetholm. As you enter the village the 'Gypsy Palace', former home of King Charles II and now an unusual holiday let, is on your left. The gypsy heritage of Yetholm also lives on in an annual procession which features a *Bari Gadgi* ('Best Boy' in the Romani language) and a *Bari Manushi* ('Best Girl').

Turn left at the village green and recross the Bowmont Water to return to Town Yetholm.

Woden Law and Dere Street

Distance 6km **Time** 2 hours
Terrain hill paths and minor road
Map OS Explorer OL16 **Access** no public
transport to the start

A frontier outpost on the edge of the
Cheviot Hills, Woden Law was the site of
an ancient hillfort adapted by the
Romans when they invaded Scotland in
around 80AD. From the 422m-high
summit you can follow the line of Dere
Street, the road into Scotland built by
General Agricola's army, which rounds
the shoulder of Woden Law as it makes its
way from York to the Firth of Forth.

The walk begins from the crossroads
just east of Towford Outdoor Education
Centre in the Upper Kale Valley, 20km
southeast of Jedburgh. There is limited
parking on the grass verge just up from
the Kale Water.

Cross the signposted stile and cut across
the corner of the field to another stile,
before following the route of Dere Street
uphill as it rises between Langside Law
and Woden Law.

Dere Street was originally known as
Agricola's Road at the time of the Roman
general's push north and was an artery
of empire, vital for communication,
military support and trade. It was still
well-used as a route into this part of
Scotland until the road over Carter Bar was
engineered in the late 1700s.

As you approach the stone shelter at
the top of the rise, bear right, then leave
Dere Street and make your way to the
summit of Woden Law. (Dere Street
continues on its way south, weaving
between the hills, to Chew Green, the site
of a vast Roman camp on the border, and
then onwards to Hadrian's Wall.)

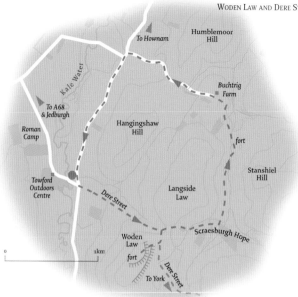

The top of the hill is a jumble of grassy ditches and ramparts and in good weather there are wonderful views of the rounded Cheviot Hills, the peaceful Kale Valley and Dere Street running north. The centre of Roman power in Scotland was at Newstead, near Melrose, and the Eildon Hills, which gave the fort of Trimontium its name, can also be seen from here.

Woden Law was used as a defensive position by local tribes long before the Roman invasion, however. The legionaries added new banks and ditches and the flat-topped outer bank probably supported catapult machines, indicating that it is most likely that troops trained here while

camped at Pennymuir further north on Dere Street, just above Towford.

Leave the summit by the same route and return to the stone shelter. Follow the wall around the sheep enclosure and continue down through the old pines before shadowing the burn down to the track which contours around the base of Langside Law. Look out on your right for another wonderfully-positioned hillfort which would once have guarded this sheltered pass through the wild hills.

The track goes around past Buchtrig Farm and then continues downhill to join a minor road which can be followed back to the start at Towford.

◀ Looking north from the summit of Woden Law

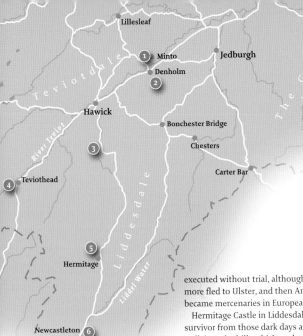

executed without trial, although many more fled to Ulster, and then America, or became mercenaries in European wars.

Hermitage Castle in Liddesdale is a survivor from those dark days and the walk into the hills which enclose it is a good introduction to this bloodily-contested buffer zone between England and Scotland.

Other walks in this chapter visit the excellent viewpoints on the summits of the Minto Hills and Ruberslaw from the villages of Minto and Denholm between Hawick and Jedburgh. Higher up Teviotdale, there is a long walk over a windswept ridge and, east of there and overlooking the tranquil Slitrig Valley, a route to the top of Penchrise Pen from the site of an old military camp. The final two walks explore quiet forest trails near the planned village of Newcastleton.

For many years the valleys of the River Teviot and the Liddel Water were caught between two warring nations, and the livelihoods of the locals suffered as devastating armies of either side swept through the countryside.

Amid this insecurity, many families – like the Armstrongs and the Elliots – defied royal authority and plundered farmsteads and villages on both sides of the border, growing wealthy and powerful before James VI finally brought their lawlessness to an end. Many Reivers were

Around Hawick and Liddesdale

The Minto Hills

Distance 7km **Time** 2 hours
Terrain hill paths, old railway bed and
minor roads **Map** OS Explorer 338
Access regular buses from Kelso to
Hawick stop in Denholm, 2km from
the start

The Minto Hills overlook the pretty
conservation village of Minto, which is
just north of the River Teviot and the
larger settlement of Denholm, midway
between Hawick and Jedburgh. There are
fine views over Teviotdale from the
rounded twin summits and the return
to the village is via the trackbed of the
old Waverley Railway Line.

Start from the William Playfair-designed
church in Minto (limited parking by the
roadside), which was the centrepiece of
the planned village commissioned by the

2nd Earl of Minto in the late 1820s. Better
known for his fine neo-classical work in
Edinburgh, which included the National
Gallery of Scotland and the Royal Scottish
Academy buildings, it was William Playfair
who made the capital city's name as
'the Athens of the North'.

Go up the road past the golf course to
reach Burncrooks Farm at the foot of the
higher of the two Minto Hills, now directly
up ahead. After another 200m, leave the
road and cross the stile on the left into the
field, then follow the path up to the saddle
between the hills.

To ascend the higher summit (276m)
take the rough and winding path on your
left that rises steeply above some crags
and then peters out as the gradient eases.
Look out for landmarks such as the three
Eildon Hills near Melrose, the rugged-

topped Ruberslaw on the other side of
Denholm, the Waterloo Monument on
Peniel Heugh, and the roof of Fatlips
Castle poking out above the wooded
summit of Minto Crags on the way up the
grassy hillside to the triangulation pillar
and memorial bench at the top.

After enjoying the view over Minto and
Denholm, return to the saddle and either
take in the other summit or contour down
around the side of the lesser hill before
crossing a stile and heading for the corner
of a strip of woodland.

Pick up the track alongside the wood
and go down to the old bridge over the
dismantled railway. This was the Waverley
Line which connected Edinburgh and
Midlothian to Hawick and Carlisle. Named
after the series of novels by Sir Walter
Scott, the line was completed in 1862 and
closed in 1969 as a result of the Beeching
Report. Part of the line, from Edinburgh to
Tweedbank, reopened in September 2015.
Make your way down onto the track bed
and head south.

Continue with the line, passing Kames
South Loch, until you reach a farm track
leading off to the right just short of the
old Hassendean Station, now a private
house. Up ahead, just beyond the bridge
over the road, is one of the last original
railway overbridges left on the line.

Follow the track down to the roads then
turn left to pass under the railway bridge
and follow the B6405 back to a junction.
Go left and follow the quiet road round
the base of the Minto Hills, enjoying a
good view of Ruberslaw and Denholm as
you return to Minto.

◀ Horses in the saddle between the Minto Hills

Ruberslaw

Distance **10km** Time **3 hours**
Terrain **hill and woodland paths,**
minor road Map **OS Explorer 331**
Access **regular buses from Kelso**
to Hawick stop in Denholm

Ruberslaw (or Rubers Law) sits between
the River Teviot and the Rule Water, an
isolated outlier of the Cheviot Hills with
a grandeur and appeal far beyond its
modest 424m height. With an excellent
view over most of Teviotdale, the hill's
volcanic summit has been home to an
Iron Age hillfort, a Roman signal station
and a stone citadel in the early Middle
Ages, as well as being a venue for illegal
Covenanter prayer meetings in the late
17th century.

Start from the village green in Denholm,
the birthplace of the remarkable John
Leyden (1775-1811), a shepherd's son who
mastered 30 languages and became a
surgeon, then a judge, in Calcutta before
falling ill and dying suddenly in Java at the
age of 36. The Leyden Monument at the
centre of the village green was built in
1861 and the thatched cottage where he
was born is on the north side.

Go along the main road (A698) out of
town past the Fox and Hounds pub and
the butcher's shop. Very soon, leave the
busy road and go up The Loaning between
houses to join a stony track signposted as
a Scottish Right of Way to Bedrule. At a
junction bear left and carry on up the track
to reach Denholmhill Wood.

Ignore a path leading off into the dark of
the trees and keep with the main track
until the signposted Borders Abbeys Way
swings left downhill. Rather than follow

the Abbeys Way, turn right and follow the edge of the field all the way along to Gled'swing Strip plantation, a strip of trees which points to the summit. (In the summer months this area is a wildwood campsite and there are several safari-style tents hidden in the trees; please be respectful of the forest campers' privacy.)

At the corner of the field, enter the woodland and pick up the path heading uphill through the trees. After a while the path bears left towards a gate; go through this and continue up the hill on a vague path which shadows the trees. Carry on along the field edge until you reach a gate at the top of the plantation.

Go through the gate and head towards the old broken-down dyke and then through some equally ancient and twisted Scots pine trees to reach the rocky top of Ruberslaw. There are some steep drops among the crags, so take care on your way to reach the summit pillar. One rocky gully is overlooked by Peden's Pulpit, where the outlawed Alexander 'Sandy' Peden from Ayrshire once stood to preach the gospel of the Covenant to his followers. The bizarre leather mask he wore as a disguise while on the run can be seen in the National Museum in Edinburgh.

When you have finished exploring the crags and enjoyed the panoramic view,

make your way back down the hill and re-enter the trees at the gate passed through earlier. At the corner of Gled'swing Strip and Denholmhill Wood, this time go left through the trees to reach a drystane dyke and a gate into a field. Follow the path, then the wide track, as it drops down to the back road into Denholm.

Rather than follow the road all the way, however, look for an opening into the wooded Denholm Dean on your left. Take the first path on the right and cross over several footbridges as you make your way to the village green.

◀ Ruberslaw above Denholm

85

Stobs Camp and Penchrise Pen

Distance 8km **Time** 2 hours (out and back) **Terrain** hill paths and tracks **Map** OS Explorer 331 **Access** regular bus from Newcastleton to Hawick passes the Stobs road end, 500m from the start

This walk to the top of Penchrise Pen is a good introduction to the quiet hill country south of Hawick. There is also some fascinating wartime history here, as the start of the walk goes through the former site of one of the largest military camps in Scotland; home, at least temporarily, to thousands of British, Polish and German servicemen and prisoners of war.

The start of the walk is 5km south of Hawick off the B6399 to Newcastleton. As the road crosses the Slitrig Water, take the minor road off to the right (if travelling from Hawick) by the war memorial. This was the entrance to Stobs Military Camp; carry on under the Barnes Viaduct to a parking area off to the left just after a cattle grid.

On the hillside to the north you can see the last surviving wooden hut from the camp which was in service for nearly 60 years. Originally a summer camp for new recruits and reservists, the site was quickly expanded to accommodate 6000 German prisoners in the early days of the First World War. More than 200 wooden huts were built in a grid pattern on the hillside below Winningtonrig Farm, with the 'streets' given German names by the prisoners, who also had their own school, library, orchestra, brass band, bakery, newspaper and hospital.

After the war Stobs returned to its previous deployment as a training camp, but at the end of the Second World War it was occupied by 2000 demobilised Polish soldiers, many of whom stayed on in the area, found jobs in farming and forestry and married local girls. By the 1950s the camp was being used less and less and it was finally dismantled in 1959.

Follow the main track uphill past the derelict farm outbuildings at Barnes and,

◀ Track to Penchrise Pen

further on, a big corrugated iron shed.
Along the way you can see
the outlines of old military
buildings and accommodation
huts. The area is also dotted
with circular hillforts and
there is a good example off
the track to the left behind a
copse of trees just after the big
shed. Between the track and
Barnes Loch, behind the
plantation down to the right,
there is also evidence of an
extensive Iron Age
settlement.

Keep straight on up the
track with Penchrise's
summit now in view,
and pass the turn down
to Penchrise Farm. Before
you arrive at the highest
point of the track between
White Hill and Penchrise, turn left
to pass the old concrete sentry post on
your way directly up the hill.

The summit was also the site of a
hillfort in the distant past, no doubt
chosen by an Iron Age chieftain for the
views over the Teviot and Slitrig Valleys.
As well as the shapely Maiden Paps rising
from the forest to the south and
distinctive Ruberslaw to the northeast,
several other prominent Border landmarks
can be identified from the top.

After enjoying the expansive view you
can return to the start by the way you

came. For a more adventurous alternative,
however, you could follow the old
Edinburgh-to-Carlisle Waverley Railway
Line which shadows the Slitrig Water. To
reach it, drop down the other side of the
hill and follow the course of the Penchrise
Burn to the farm track and then work your
way east over farmland to the line. Follow
the sometimes overgrown railway bed
north, turning off to the left not long after
passing Stobs Castle to return to the start.

Teviothead and the Three Stanes

Distance 14km **Time** 4 hours
Terrain minor road, access tracks and
open hillside **Map** OS Explorer 331
Access buses from Langholm to Hawick
will stop at Teviothead on request

This long walk over the hills south
of Hawick starts from the spot where
one of the most notorious Border Reivers
met his end, passes a hillside memorial to
a local motorcycling hero and finishes by
a monument to a songwriting minister
inspired by this rolling landscape.

Start from Teviothead Parish Church on
the minor road signposted for Carlenrig
off the A7, almost halfway between
Hawick and Langholm.

On the other side of the road from the
church is the grave of Johnnie Armstrong
of Gilnockie, a charismatic rogue also
known as Black Jock, who terrorised
Northumberland and Cumbria, as well as
his native Borderlands, in the early 16th
century. An information board by the
stone which marks his grave tells the

story of how he was tricked by the teenage
King James V – under pressure from his
uncle Henry VIII to rid the Borders of the
troublesome Reivers – into a meeting
which ended with bold Johnnie, and
many of his followers, hanging from
nearby trees.

Head up the minor road and carry on all
the way along Caerlan Rig, the ridge
between the infant River Teviot and
Limiecleuch Burn. On the way there is a
more recent memorial to Steve 'Hizzy'
Hislop, a Hawick-born motorcycle racer
who died in a helicopter crash on a
nearby hillside.

After the road finally drops down to
cross the Teviot, go through the gate

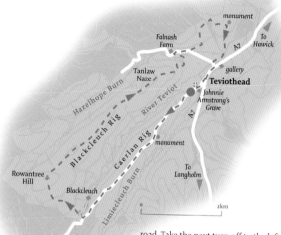

signed for Blackcleuch, then turn left through another gate and follow the track which takes you up onto the hillside. Go up the track shadowing the burn until it fades away, then bear right and follow the fence to the top of Rowantree Hill.

Keep with the fence and then the dyke over the high ground of Blackcleuch Rig and when the dyke eventually turns sharply left, keep straight on to pass by a sheep enclosure and head up over Tanlaw Naze. Come down on the northeast side of the hill, passing the communications mast, and follow the winding access track down towards Falnash Farm.

Cross the footbridge over Hazelhope Burn and turn right when you get to the

road. Take the next turn-off to the left at Birkiebrae before leaving the track on a grassy path to head towards an old quarry. Go through a gate beyond the quarry and cross the fields, aiming for the top corner of the forestry above Parkhead Cottage. Cross the Dryden Burn and skirt around the forestry before bearing east towards the A7.

The Henry Scott Riddell Monument, also known as the Colterscleuch Monument, was erected in 1874 in memory of the local minister who lived in a nearby cottage. Several of his compositions, including 'Scotland Yet' and 'The Dowie Dens o'Yarrow' are still performed by folk artists. With the trunk road in view below, drop down the hillside and follow the track down to the bridge over the Teviot. Turn right and return to the start with a short walk along the roadside verge.

◄ The Henry Scott Riddell Monument

Hermitage Castle and Hill

Distance 5km **Time** 2 hours
Terrain rough and sometimes boggy
hillside **Map** OS Explorer 324 **Access** buses
from Hawick stop at Hermitage village,
1km from the castle

Hermitage Castle, 'the strength of
Liddesdale', is a gaunt 14th-century
stronghold steeped in dark legend and
bloody Borders history. A short but
rugged route explores the area around the
enigmatic castle and provides a better
sense of its place in the local landscape as
well as Borders history.

Start from the bridge over the Hermitage
Water (with roadside car park) and head
towards the castle. Leaving the tour for
later, go through the gate on the left, just
before the Historic Scotland kiosk, to reach

the open hillside. The ground is rough
most of the way to the top and there is no
clear path or shelter, so make sure you are
properly prepared.

The only prominent feature on the
hillside ahead is a sheep enclosure: head
slightly northeast of that, picking up sheep
trods as you go. After a good bit of huffing
and puffing you will reach the tumbled
remains of the White Dyke, a massive deer
enclosure built with limestone blocks,
which once curved all around the hillside.

Looking back down to the castle you can
see its strategic importance; it would be
difficult for any invading force to pass
through this vast buffer zone between the
lawless Debatable Lands of the south and
the more civilised north without
attracting attention. Being so near the

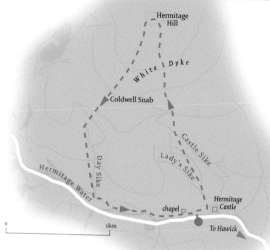

English border also made the castle a valuable prize and unsurprisingly Hermitage has been called 'the guardhouse of Britain's bloodiest valley'.

As you make your way over the rough ground, spare a thought, too, for poor old Mary Queen of Scots who stumbled into a marsh and caught a fever whilst making an arduous journey over these hills from Jedburgh and back again the same day. Her dash to comfort the Earl of Bothwell after he was badly wounded in a fight with some local Reivers was scandalous as well as reckless – she was married to Lord Darnley at the time.

The rewards for your effort as you pull up onto the summit plateau are wonderful views over the surrounding countryside with Din Fell prominent to the south. To descend, follow the fenceline southwest

from the rounded summit until you pick up a well-constructed stone dyke which carries on south to the Hermitage Water. From here it is a leisurely stroll along the riverbank to reach the ruins of a 13th-century chapel and graveyard with the castle just beyond.

It is worth visiting the castle just to experience its chilling atmosphere – it is a brutal construction and there are plenty of grisly tales attached to it, many of which were the work of the ballad writer Dr John Leyden, a friend of Sir Walter Scott. He elaborated on its dark history from semi-barbarous feudal days to produce grim tales which have become confused with reality over the passing years. All the same, make sure you leave before it gets dark.

◀ Hermitage Castle

Priest Hill

Distance 4km **Time** 1 hour
Terrain clear paths, sometimes boggy in
parts **Map** OS Explorer 324 **Access** buses
from Hawick stop in Newcastleton,
4.5km from Priesthill car park

This is a little gem of a Liddesdale walk
with easy paths, great views, an Iron Age
fort and a wildlife hide from which to spot
badgers in the evenings.

The Forestry Commission car park
(no charge) at Priesthill is 1km further
along the minor road from the 7Stanes
trailhead at Dykecrofts (well-signposted
from the main road through the village
of Newcastleton).

Several colour-coded trails start from
the car park; the route to the wildlife
hide at the top of Priest Hill is the
purple-arrowed Viewpoint Trail.

From the car park, cross the little
wooden footbridge over the Whithaugh
Burn. Long ago this was forded by a
turnpike road and the spot was said to be
haunted by fairies and the spirits of the
departed from the local churchyard; a sign
supposedly once hung here which read
'No Road This Way After Dark'. The ponds
to the left are home to dragonflies in
summer and the short trail around them
is great for children.

Follow the path up the hillside and
off to the left and keep with it as it weaves
its way round the side of the hill. After

◀ Looking east from Priest Hill

passing a couple of benches, the purple waymarkers direct you to make a sharp right turn for a short pull to the cleared summit.

A concrete trig post marks the highest point (205m) of the walk, but the effort in getting to the top is not fully rewarded until you make your way through a tunnel of trees to enjoy a panoramic view over Liddesdale.

Sir Walter Scott described this landscape well when he said that the hills have 'no pretensions to magnificence of height or to romantic shapes, nor do their smooth swelling slopes exhibit either rocks or woods. Yet the view is wild, solitary, and pleasingly rural'.

After exploring the wildlife hide on the hillside, carry on with the waymarked path to return to the start, looking out for the huge circular defensive ditches of an Iron Age hillfort on the way.

B6357

Liddel Water

fort

hide

0   500m

Priest Hill

Crossgill Sike

Whithaugh Burn

Dykecrofts
Plantation

ford

Priesthill
Knowe

To Newcastleton   Dykecrofts

Newcastleton Forest and the Border Stane

Distance 8km **Time** 2 hours
Terrain solid forest roads all the way
Map OS Explorer 324 **Access** buses from
Hawick stop in Newcastleton, 3.5km
from Dykecrofts car park

The vast Newcastleton Forest in
Liddesdale combines with the even
larger Kielder Forest of Northumberland
to make this the biggest plantation area
in Britain. There are several walks of
varying length signposted in the forest;
this easygoing route follows the Linns
Trail through an idyllic wooded valley
full of wildlife to reach the Border Stane,
one of seven sculptures that can be
found in the 7Stanes mountain biking
trail centres of Southern Scotland.

The Forestry Commission car park
(no charge) and information centre at
Dykecrofts is well signposted from the
main road through the village of
Newcastleton. Several colour-coded
walking trails start from here, and also
from the Priesthill car park 1km further
along the minor road.

From Dykecrofts, follow the All Trails
signpost and head up the hill on a
well-surfaced forest road to enter the
plantation. Newcastleton is a 7Stanes
mountain biking centre and there are
several narrow trails weaving through
the trees, as well as a skills area which can
be glimpsed off to the right as you follow
the red waymarkers into the forest.

There are great views of the high open moorland of Liddesdale on this early stage of the walk. Before the conifers were first planted following World War One and the formation of the Forestry Commission in 1919, all of the valley would have looked like this, and dotted around the forest you can see the broken-down remains of old stells and rough bothies which once provided shelter for the sheep and shepherds.

After 1km the red trail drops down to the right and meanders through an area of older mixed woodland to cross the Tweeden Burn. With towering trees all around, the road follows the burn back up the other side of the valley to reach the Border Stane at a junction.

Commissioned as part of the 7Stanes mountain biking initiative, this is one of seven sculptures located alongside trails deep in various forests of Southern Scotland. The words of William Blake's *Jerusalem* are inscribed on the side facing England and those of Robert Burns' *Auld Lang Syne* on the other – a hole in the middle allows friendly fellow Britons to shake hands through the middle.

From here, go left and follow the red markers along the forest road to reach the abandoned cottage at Tweedenhead. Cross the wooden bridge over the burn and follow the open forest road back to the start at Dykecrofts.

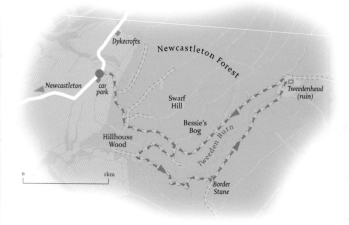

◀ The Border Stane

Index